ALASKA
NATIVE WAYS

ALASKA
NATIVE WAYS

WHAT THE ELDERS HAVE TAUGHT US

PHOTOGRAPHY BY **ROY CORRAL**

INTRODUCTION BY **WILL MAYO**

ESSAYISTS

DIANA CAMPBELL, Athabascan ▪ WALKIE CHARLES, Yup'ik

RUTHIE LEE TATQAVIN RAMOTH-SAMPSON, Iñupiat

PHILIP KELLY, Aleut ▪ NORA MARKS DAUENHAUER, Tlingit

SVEN HAAKANSON Jr., Alutiiq ▪ DAVID BOXLEY, Tsimshian

GEORGE NOONGWOOK, Siberian Yupik

JEANE BREINIG, Haida ▪ DUNE LANKARD, Eyak

GRAPHIC ARTS CENTER PUBLISHING®

To my lifelong love, Kim, for being my beacon of hope during uncharted journeys;
to my brother, Denis, for unfailing support; and to new and old friends who
opened their hearts and homes across Alaska—thank you.

—R.C.

Photos © MMII by Roy Corral, except author photos as credited below
Text © MMII by contributors as credited in each chapter

Map base used with permission of the Alaska Native Language Center. To obtain a copy, contact ANLC at (907) 474-7874 or e-mail fyanlp@uaf.edu.

Library of Congress Cataloging-in-Publication Data

Corral, Roy, 1946-
  Alaska Native ways : what the elders have taught us / photography by Roy Corral.
    p. cm.
Includes bibliographical references and index.
  ISBN 1-55868-500-6 (hardback)
  1. Eskimo aged. 2. Eskimo philosophy. 3. Eskimos—Social life and customs. 4. Indian aged—Alaska. 5. Indian philosophy—Alaska. 6. Indians of North America—Alaska—Social life and customs. I. Title.
  E99.E7 B764 2002
  305.897'1—dc21   2002001717

Graphic Arts Center Publishing®
An imprint of Graphic Arts Center Publishing Co.
P.O. Box 10306, Portland, OR 97296-0306
(503) 226-2402
www.gacpc.com

President: Charles M. Hopkins
Associate Publisher: Douglas A. Pfeiffer
Editorial Staff: Timothy W. Frew, Ellen Harkins Wheat, Tricia Brown, Jean Andrews,
    Kathy Matthews, Jean Bond-Slaughter
Project Editor: Martha Bristow
Production Staff: Richard L. Owsiany, Heather Doornink
Design: Elizabeth Watson
Map: Marge Mueller, Gray Mouse Graphics

Author photographs courtesy of the authors. Page 49, Ruthie Lee Tatqavin Ramoth-Sampson photo by © James Magdanz. Page 125, Jeane Breinig © photo by Nuen Lui Studio. Page 138, Dune Lankard photo by © Roy Corral.

Photographs: Cover, background: A party of Siberian Yupik hunters; cover inset photo and page 1: Lorraine Williams and daughter Gwendolyn Shetters in her fancy parka. Page 2: Savoonga whale hunters on a journey across St. Lawrence Island. Page 3: Whale's skull and jaw bones bleach in the sun, St. Lawrence Island. Page 5: Atka Island dancer. Pages 8-9: Whaling camp on shore ice. Page 144: An Iñupiat girl, Albertha Wilson, cuddles her husky puppy.

Printed in Hong Kong
Bound by Lincoln & Allen in Portland, Oregon, United States of America

ACKNOWLEDGMENTS

Jim & Chris Rowe of Bering Air, Craig & Syd George, Robert Lewis & Kirsten Bey, Joseph Oscar Jr., Chester & Sally Noongwook, Wayne & Toni Hewson, Wesley & Sharon Henry, Sarah James, Gideon James, Billy Rivers, Harley Sundown, Joe & Belen Cook, Dune Lankard, the Noongwook family, Savoonga Village Council, Oliver Leavitt & Family, Eugene Brower, Jim & Karin Gillis, Ed & Jackie Debevec, Lisa Drew, Kenneth Marsh, Jack & Iris Huckleberry, Geoff & Marie Carroll, Gambell IRA, Patricia Watts, Sheryl Sharp-DeBoard, Cheryl Richardson, Steve & Melody Leask, Dr. Peter Mjos & Karen Ruud, Michelle Amundsen, Cindy & Greg Bombeck, Kelly Bostian, Bill Williams, Lindbergh & Lydia Bergman, Virginia & Stanley Ned, Jerry & Rose Domnick, Charlie & Geraldine Fairbanks, Chief Peter John, Kathy & Dr. Bill Roberts, Carleen Jack, Thelma & Darlene Kaganak, Edmond & Delma Apassingok, Margaret Nelson, Barbara MacManus, Tuntutuliak Village Council, Dr. Denis Corral, Bristol Bay Area Health Corp., the Killer Whale Clan, Beverly Lewanski, Bonnie Bernholz, Robbie Graham, Lynn & Carol Norstadt, Bill & Cathy Fliris, Pat & Lorene Moore, Velma & Larry Schaeffer, Andy Hall, Jennifer Williams, Larry & Moses Dirks, Minnie Gray, Katharine Cleveland, Mercy Cleveland, Venita & Steve Pilz, Gertrude Svarny, Pat Lekanoff-Gregory, Gerard & Judy Helgesen, Mel & Ruth Booth, Kid Helgesen, Richard Peterson, Pam McCamy, Louis & Annette Thompson, Don & Jenny Kratzer, Cheryl Richardson, The Rasmusson Museum, Anchorage Museum of History & Art, Alaska Federation of Natives, Alaska Native Heritage Center, Fairbanks North Star Borough School district, Fairbanks Native Education Association, Alaska Native Knowledge Network, Alaska Native Language Center.

To Doug Pfeiffer of Graphic Arts Center Publishing®, thank you for believing in and supporting this endeavor. Our gratitude extends especially to editors Tim Frew, Tricia Brown, Ellen Harkins Wheat, and Martha Bristow for their invaluable direction and tender nudging. Thanks to Sara Juday and Angie Zbornik. Also, I am once again stunned by the magic of designer Elizabeth Watson. Thank you, all.

C O N T E N T S

ALASKA

ALEUT

ALUTIIQ

ATHABASCAN

EYAK

HAIDA

IÑUPIAT

SIBERIAN YUPIK

TLINGIT

TSIMSHIAN

YUP'IK

St. Matthew
Island

Pribilof
Islands

Aleutian Islands

ARCTIC
OCEAN

RUSSIA
UNITED STATES

Big
Diomede

Little
Diomede

KOTZEBUE

ARCTIC CIRCLE

SAVOONGA

St.
Lawrence
Island

*Bering
Sea*

EMMONAK

VENETIE

TANANA

FAIRBANKS

Nunivak
Island

ALASKA

UNITED STATES
CANADA

*Lake
Iliamna*

ANCHORAGE

CORDOVA

EGEGIK

N
W   E
S

Eyak

MILES
0   100   200   300

0   100   200   300
KILOMETERS

Kodiak
Island

KODIAK

Gulf of Alaska

PACIFIC   OCEAN

JUNEAU

CANADA
UNITED STATES

Prince of Wales
Island

HYDABURG

METLAKATLA

Annette Island

9

Preface:
Gratitude for These Gifts

ROY CORRAL

I stood at the doorway of Katie John's log cabin in Mentasta Village, Alaska, one spring more than three decades ago. Surrounded by craggy mountains that left me breathless, I marveled at the spectacular surroundings as I waited. The wooden door creaked open, and Katie welcomed me into her simple home, which was about thirty miles southwest of Tok. A hitchhiker with a guitar and a banjo, I was a stranger to her, but I had provided entertainment at a nearby gathering for most of the previous night, and she had invited me over for a visit. That morning Katie had been making breakfast, and the aroma of coffee filled the warm room. Now a revered elder and an activist for Native rights, Katie was then a lively woman in her middle years. Despite my fatigue, her easy conversation about the Athabascan way of life captivated me. She shared stories of gathering autumn berries, catching her winter's supply of red and silver salmon from the Copper River, hunting moose along lazy sloughs, and trapping nearby forests and lakes for fur. In one of the back rooms, stiff bundles of marten, lynx, fox, and beaver lay neatly stacked like cordwood.

As Katie cradled a wolf pelt, she spoke wistfully about her beloved Native ways, fearing that day when her ancient traditions might be forever lost. After all, social and economic changes spawned by the trans-Alaska oil pipeline loomed ahead for Natives and non-Natives alike. A surge of modern pioneers like me had cast a whole new factor into the natural resources equation. Increased competition and regulations would surely tighten the snare. Surprisingly, Katie John offered to take me on for a one-year apprenticeship to learn the old ways of her Athabascan heritage. But in the foolishness of youth, I thanked her and gave an excuse, explaining my dream to explore the wilds of Alaska and to find a remote land parcel that I could call my own.

Within three years, I had staked a forty-acre homestead barely north of the Arctic Circle in the Brooks Range. During sporadic seasonal stints, I tried my hand for more than a decade at living off the land, often thinking of Katie as I peeled bark from spruce logs for my small cabin, cured moose meat for winter, plucked blueberries from fall mountainsides, and ran a team of sled dogs in winter to check my modest trapline. I realized that a trapper I was not, and abandoned that idea while gaining newfound respect for Katie and others of her spirit.

Instead, I found that words and pictures became my tools of choice to help document and preserve the Native ways of life and the values that generations have lived by. I have traveled extensively with and without cameras from Barrow in the north to Ketchikan in the south, and from the Canadian border in the east to the Aleutian Islands in the far west. Everyone I met embraced the best of their Native heritage and traditions while weaving old with new. They also embraced me in welcome and gladly opened their homes to share their daily lives. Many allowed me to briefly become a member of their families—hauling water, cooking on propane stoves, stoking wood fires, sampling dried fish dipped in seal oil over coffee and conversation— and then to become the fly-on-the-wall observer documenting their proud, individual ways of living in community and crafting a living from the land, rivers, and seas.

In one of the most important lessons of my travels, I learned to understand the critical importance of wild meat, fresh fish, berries, and wild greens for food and medicine—and Native identity—in some of the most remote regions of Alaska. I lost count of how often someone said, "Out there is our grocery store," referring to the surrounding wild land or marine environment.

In *Alaska Native Ways*, I hope to take the reader to some of the places where I have been and beyond, where few outsiders have had the opportunity to go. We wanted people to hear Native voices from throughout the state, from Kotzebue up north, to Saint Lawrence Island in the icy Bering Sea, to Metlakatla in the southern reaches. We pondered how to show the range of experiences and traditions among these writers and then discovered the Alaska Native Values for the Curriculum on a website called the Alaska Native Knowledge Network. The site includes lists of personal and community values that several Native groups cite as most important to their people. With cosponsorship from the Fairbanks Native Education Association, educators had also assembled a list of ten traditional values that are common to all Alaska Native cultures—values such as respect for elders, the importance of sharing, patience, careful living, and knowing who you are. With the association's permission, the editors of *Alaska Native Ways* invited a writer from each of ten Native groups to address one of those values within the framework of his or her experience. Together with photographs, the essays help create a sense of how today's Native peoples are drawing strength and guidance from ancient traditional ways—what has been passed along by the elders—as they move into the future.

As a photojournalist, I have attempted to capture the moments that unfolded before me, always guided by the uncompromising standard to frame cultural truth uncluttered by either internal or external influences. The choice to photograph someone wearing traditional regalia or jeans and sweatshirt always belonged to the individual. For those years spent with deliberate intent to document photographically Alaska's Native ways, I can only say thank you to the countless Native people across the state whose hospitality and generosity transcended all cultural differences between us.

From my perspective behind the lens, it seemed I was always the observer. Yet that surely wasn't the case. I remember the time MaryAnn Sundown, a Yup'ik elder from Scammon Bay, was keeping an eye on me, too, as she wove an intricate grass basket. My shoes were at the front door, as is the custom, and I was working in stocking feet, moving around her from every angle, my lens close up to focus on the dexterous motion of her hands. Then MaryAnn excused herself in Yup'ik, waving her nimble hands for me to wait a moment. As I gathered my gear, she returned and, smiling up from her shy eyes, she handed me a pair of thick socks. I looked down and saw what she had already seen—big toes poking through blown-out socks.

In Native tradition, nothing escapes notice. Eventually, this accumulated treasure of ancient knowledge practiced in modern times is the legacy that each generation hands to the next.

The photographs in this book embody my gratitude for all that has been graciously given to me over the years, beginning with a cup of coffee at Katie John's cabin.

Common values

With cosponsorship from the Fairbanks Native Education Association, educators had also assembled a list of ten traditional values . . . such as respect for elders, the importance of sharing, patience, careful living, and knowing who you are.

▲ SCAMMON BAY ELDER MARYANN "ARNAUCUAQ" SUNDOWN AT WORK ON A YUP'IK BASKET.

◄ TLINGIT TOTEM.

Introduction:
Anchoring Values

WILL MAYO

▲ VILLAGERS FROM ALLAKAKET, HUGHES, HUSLIA, AND OTHER ATHABASCAN VILLAGES CELEBRATE A POTLATCH AT THE ALLAKAKET COMMUNITY HALL.

We danced hard, sweating, locked in an ancient battle. I, the Athabascan Indian, and Ben Nageak, the Iñupiat Eskimo (and then mayor of the North Slope Borough), were fully engaged in the struggle of our lives. We faced each other on the dance floor of the village gathering hall, sometimes touching arms in our closeness. Our eyes were wary and quick, cutting hard with each new move of challenge from the other. The other dancers left the floor, the better to enjoy the impromptu sparring of the "warriors." Our dancing had become the depiction of an ancient contest between our peoples, and we were center stage.

As we darted toward and then away from the imaginary skirmish line, the gathered people hooted and howled their approval, singing and drumming all the louder. After a few minutes of "deadly combat," our antics turned to the comical. Laughter filled the room at our parody of aboriginal machismo. The song ended in a crescendo and we embraced each other in brotherly mirth. The faces of the villagers shone with pleasure as our fun became theirs. In millennia past, our peoples, the Iñupiat of the North and the Athabascan of Interior Alaska, had fought over territorial borders. Now, our cultural expressions blended in a simple, yet profound, new realization. At the dawn of a fresh millennium we still had a foundation upon which to face modern challenges. Our cultures had brought us this far against imponderable odds, and they would carry us farther still into an unknown future.

We danced during a traditional potlatch gathering (ceremonial feast) in honor of Chief Walter Charlie of Copper Center, a respected Athabascan elder who had recently passed away. Ben and I honored him with the blending of our traditional dances. He had honored us by passing on his cultural knowledge and helping to make the "Native way" a continuum of anchoring values. As modern Native leaders of our respective peoples, Ben and I had often felt the weight of our responsibilities. As we walked off the dance floor to a thunderous standing ovation, we both felt ourselves lifted by the spirit of our deceased elder. It is because of people like him that we can sing and dance the ancient songs at all. We were both determined that the continuum would not be broken during our short sojourn in this world. The success of our peoples today may be aided by e-mail, telephones, jets, and cars, but the Native way continues to be our identity and touchstone.

Over the years, as I have traveled among and worked with the various First Nations peoples of Alaska, I have often been struck by the many similarities in our cultures. As an Athabascan child, I became aware of the differences between the various Native peoples and did not realize that there were far more instances of shared values and beliefs. All too often we are tempted to accentuate our differences while failing to see the commonalities we share.

It is clear that many of our beliefs and values spring from close Native ties to the land and creatures over multiple thousands of years. Native people share these ancient connections to Alaska, which are evidenced in part by the cultural manifestations depicted in this book. I believe that there is much to learn for anyone who will respectfully observe.

I am delighted to discover striking similarities among Native cultures. For example, I had a discussion with a Yup'ik friend about the respectful care and handling of animals and fish that are taken for food. In the old ways it is believed that the spirit of the creature remains in the vicinity of its body for a period of time and observes how it is treated by the persons who handle it. Proper handling is rewarded, while disrespectful or careless handling carries potentially dangerous consequences. In my Koyukon Athabascan culture, this is part of what I like to call the "Hutlaanee Code." This code guides our people in proper, respectful interactions with the world around us. It is the basis of our law and our instructional code for successful living. I was therefore intrigued by the close beliefs held by other Native peoples.

Of course, the similarities are easily matched by the ways in which the tribes differ. These differences are seen in any number of striking examples, such as language, dance styles, clothing styles, and art, to name a few. Still, these are to me just different manifestations of the same core values that bind together Alaska's Native peoples. When I first read the pieces in this book, I became excited that these shared values found voice through Native-written essays, accompanied by the inspiring work of photographer Roy Corral. I have enjoyed Roy's work ever since we collaborated on a project involving First Traditional Chief Peter John of Minto in the Tanana Chiefs region. Roy's portraits of the Traditional Chief were powerful images of the man in his environment.

I know that Roy's work in this book will transport readers beyond these pages and into an Alaska few are blessed to experience firsthand. The essayists, all Natives from around this great land, have captured elements of our cultures that convey the warmth and love of a people for their ancient homelands and waters. Honorable and respectful depictions of our Alaska Native ways are refreshing and welcome. I know there is so much that is lovely and admirable in Native cultures that has not found adequate expression in printed media: love for elders, delightful humor, respect for the land and animals, sharing, and insightful spirituality. I am proud and honored to introduce this work, and I pray a blessing on you as you enjoy these vignettes of the beauty and splendor of Alaska Native ways.

Will Mayo is a tribal member of the Athabascan village of Tanana and now lives in Fairbanks. He travels throughout Alaska as Senior Advisor for Rural Policy for Alaska Governor Tony Knowles. Will is married to Yvonne, his wife of twenty-five years, and has three children and one grandchild.

Potlatch gathering

The success of our peoples today may be aided by e-mail, telephones, jets, and cars, but the Native way continues to be our identity and touchstone.

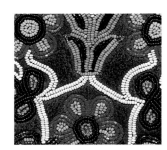

The Athabascan Indian people of the Interior region live in communities as large as Alaska's second-largest city—Fairbanks—to small, remote villages along great rivers. Their ancestors were a seminomadic people who learned how to survive through feast and famine in a region where Fahrenheit temperatures could range from ninety degrees above zero in summers to seventy degrees below in winters. Athabascans have always hunted moose, caribou, bear, and smaller game, and fished for salmon, whitefish, and other fish species. Many families rely heavily on hunting and fishing, even though every village has a little store, and city residents can choose among several supermarkets.

Athabascan artists are known for their work with beads, quills, and dentalium on moosehide clothing, slippers, baby-carrying straps, gun cases, dolls, and jewelry. In past times, there was extensive trade among the people and with neighboring peoples. Then and now, potlatch celebrations included gift giving, dancing, fiddling, singing, speeches, and feasting.

Athabascans are subdivided into eleven groups in Alaska, with about twenty more in Canada. Although all Athabascans share common traditions and ways of living, each group has its own language and rules about how individuals should conduct themselves.

Show Respect to Others—
Each Person Has a Special Gift

◆

DIANA CAMPBELL

⊙

Time has a way of blowing chaff from my memories of the

people I have buried until nothing is left but the essence of

who they were. To this day, my mother's sweet goodness

cloaks me in the most comfortable fashion, like a gentle

▲ AUTUMN COLOR SWEEPS ACROSS THE HILLSIDES AROUND HUGHES,
LOCATED ON THE KOYUKUK RIVER.

◄ CHIEF PETER JOHN OF MINTO IS HONORED FOR HIS WISE LEADERSHIP.

15

▲ CURIOUS CHILDREN FROM ARCTIC VILLAGE PEER OUT AT A NEW FACE IN THEIR VILLAGE.

► ON HIS FIRST MOOSE HUNT WITH THE OLDER MEN OF HIS FAMILY, JERRALD JOHN DISCOVERS BEAR TRACKS ALONG THE CHANDALAR RIVER, NORTH OF ARCTIC VILLAGE.

summer breeze. Of course, she was much more than that, but after all of these years since her death, her sweetness is what remains and is what I tell my children about.

It was from my mother that I learned about my grandfather, John Fredson. He died when my mother was a girl of eight, but he figured prominently in my life through the stories I heard of him. Whether it was a family story about him cooking my grandmother's favorite meal of salmon bellies and potatoes, or an account of him walking hundreds of miles to gain support for the Venetie Indian Reservation, the memories of his personal strength and his service to others are what remain. That is how I know him. My grandfather believed the value of his life was as a trailblazer, and he pushed ahead, but he always showed respect for other people.

My grandfather was Gwich'in Athabascan, born sometime around 1895 near the Sheenjek River, a wild waterway that drains south from the Brooks Range into the Yukon. The Alaska Gold Rush was on, and it brought changes to the Athabascan way of life. My great-grandfather left my grandfather with missionaries from time to time, and one of these, the adventuresome Episcopal Archdeacon Hudson Stuck, declared him to be a bright boy who deserved special attention and education. My grandfather accompanied Stuck on many of his travels by boat or by dogsled. One of those trips brought my grandfather to the foot of Denali to keep camp while Stuck, Harry Karstens, Bob Tatum, and Walter Harper made the first successful climb of North America's highest peak.

A young man of about seventeen, my grandfather waited alone in the wilderness for nearly a month while the men made their climb. Fire had destroyed a supply cache

Respect

My grandfather pushed ahead,

but he always showed respect

for other people.

▶ A PARTY OF YOUNG HUNTERS USE
BINOCULARS AND SCOPES TO SCAN THE
CHANDALAR RIVER VALLEY, LOOKING FOR
MOOSE TO SUSTAIN THE FAMILY FOR THE
NEXT YEAR.

▼ TRAVELING ON THE KOYUKUK RIVER IN
SEPTEMBER, McGARRETT JOHN KEEPS HIS EARS
WARM WITH A WOLF-FUR HAT.

▲ PLAYING AT FISH CAMP, A YOUNG GIRL FROM HUGHES BECOMES ENTANGLED AS SALMON DRY ON THE SPRUCE POLE ABOVE HER.

and left the group short of rations, and my grandfather hunted to feed himself and Stuck's seven sled dogs. The climbers left him a small portion of canned milk and sugar for his tea, but my grandfather decided to save it for the men when they returned. My grandfather was so grateful to the archdeacon for including him that he wanted to do something for the man, who was nearly fifty.

It was not unusual for young Athabascan men to deny themselves food or drink to endure long hunts. I'm sure this was something my grandfather was taught. Stuck was so impressed by my grandfather's milk-and-sugar fast that he wrote about it in *Ascent of Denali,* his book about the climb. That was one of the first stories I heard about my

Special Gifts

Certain individuals had to learn the white man's ways and then return to work among their people.

◄ SELINA ALEXANDER IS AN EXPERT AT BEADWORK, AS WERE MANY GENERATIONS BEFORE HER.

▼ BILL WILLIAMS CAREFULLY SKINS A MOOSE HEAD. THE SALVAGED MEAT WILL BE USED IN A GENEROUS POT OF MOOSE-HEAD SOUP.

grandfather. Many times when I've been in trouble, I've thought about the courage and discipline displayed by the young man alone at the base of the mountain and how much it meant to those weary men after their arduous climb to have fresh meat and hot, sweet, creamy tea.

Another story I heard often was how my grandfather became the first Athabascan to graduate from college. He was much older than the average freshman when he enrolled in 1922 at Sewanee, The University of the South, in Tennessee. Stuck believed that the way Alaska Natives could survive the changes brought by Western expansion was through education. Certain individuals had to learn the white man's ways and then return to work among their people. Stuck and others thought my grandfather had the ability to succeed at college and then return to serve the Gwich'in.

My grandfather must have believed that, too. He became a modern hunter, and armed with the power of a good education, he secured Gwich'in land nearly thirty years before Congress passed the Alaska Native Claims Settlement Act in 1971. I was

always proud to hear this story as a child, and my grandfather's accomplishment pushed me to finish college. As an adult, however, I've been able to look at my grandfather's achievement from a different angle.

It must have been difficult for a full-blooded Indian to attend a Southern school, even if it was a prestigious institution that focused on learning, achievement, and good manners. Most of the people at the school liked my grandfather immediately and even invited him to their homes during breaks. But not everyone liked him. During my grandfather's freshman year, while he was in his dorm room studying, a rather obnoxious young man made a nasty comment about his Athabascan heritage. A roommate remembered that my grandfather did not move, but the roommate saw the back of his neck redden.

Finally, my grandfather put down his book, got up, and walked over to the offender. He placed his hand on the young man's shoulder and said, "George, you know you are my friend."

I've wondered what would have happened if my grandfather had punched the guy. But John Fredson had much to lose. It took a lot of hard work on his part and that of his teachers for him to come from the wilds of Alaska to that college dorm room. He was attending the school on a special scholarship, and people who had faith in his abilities had sacrificed for him to get there. It was not part of Athabascan tradition to waste those efforts on a loss of control. If he had gotten into a fight, it is likely administrators would have focused on the display of temper, not on the circumstances.

◄ COURTNEY MOORE HARVESTS SALMON FROM HER FAMILY'S FISHWHEEL ON THE YUKON RIVER NEAR TANANA.

▲ KATHLEEN CARLO-KENDALL CREATES AN ICE SCULPTURE FOR THE WORLD ICE ART CHAMPIONSHIPS IN FAIRBANKS.

I believe my grandfather understood that beneath the bully façade lies a miserable person who needs redemption. I think maybe he also wanted to teach George that he had value, and perhaps he hoped that George would take the gift of respect given to him that day and pass it along to others. I don't know what happened to George, or if he ever learned temperance for himself, but in that instance he was met by something stronger than his own misery.

My grandfather stayed in school, and despite occasional financial hardships and illness, he graduated in 1930. Later, back in Alaska, he accepted a job as a school-teacher in Venetie. It was at this time that he began his work toward forming the Venetie Indian Reservation, making sure that his people retained their land. Today the people of Arctic Village and Venetie hold full title to 1.8 million acres of Alaska land.

I am not the only one who remembers my grandfather. The chiefs of the reservation lands invoke his name at gatherings, and Venetie schoolchildren write essays about this man who sacrificed so much for them. I tell my own children about him.

I think some people believe that showing deference to others is a weakness. My grandfather, even though I never met him, taught me that respect for others takes great strength of character. While the memory of my mother buoys me, the memory of my grandfather gives me backbone.

◄ HAZEL AMBROSE CHECKS ON MOOSE MEAT AND SALMON STRIPS HANGING IN HER SMOKEHOUSE.

▲ STANLEY NED HANDS OUT WOLF FUR RUFFS AS GIFTS DURING A MEMORIAL POTLATCH IN ALLAKAKET.

Diana Campbell is a tribal member of the Native village of Venetie. She grew up in Fairbanks and resides there with her husband, Mack, and three daughters. Diana is a graduate of the University of Alaska Fairbanks and is the business reporter at the Fairbanks Daily News-Miner.

YUP'IK

The Yup'ik Eskimo people of southwest Alaska are Alaska's largest Native group, and almost half speak their Native language. The people live in a broad region that includes tundra, forests, coastline, and river delta, stretching from the villages of Golovin and Elim on the south side of the Seward Peninsula, down the coast to the Alaska Peninsula and including Nunivak Island. Most villages are either on the coast or along rivers.

In English, the word *yup'ik* means "real person." The Siberian Yupik people of St. Lawrence Island are not part of the Yup'ik group of southwestern Alaska. Even the spelling of "yupik," with or without an apostrophe, shows two different ways of pronouncing the same word.

The Yup'ik people are known for their artistic expressions, such as drumming, dancing, storytelling, and carvings, ranging from elaborate dance masks to delicate ivory figures. Every season brings with it a reason to celebrate: a time to gather berries; a time to work at fish camp, drying and smoking fish; a time to look for big game, or seals, or ducks; a time to remember a person who is gone or to observe a holy day. Many Yup'ik people are members of a church body such as Russian Orthodox, Moravian, Assembly of God, or Roman Catholic. As with other Native groups, some people retain the spiritual knowledge from the time before missionaries came to Alaska, and quietly practice the old ways.

See Connections—
All Things Are Related

◆

WALKIE CHARLES

⦿

Every Yup'ik child is introduced to the natural environment—

the elements water, air, and earth—at a very early age by parents

and caregivers. I remember as a young boy how my father

would wake me in the morning and say, *Makluten cella paqesgu,*

▲ BERTHA OHMAN PICKS WILD CELERY NEAR THE VILLAGE OF TUNUNAK.

◄ AN EARLY SUMMER CATCH OF SALMON DRIES ON RACKS IN HOOPER BAY, A
VILLAGE ON NELSON ISLAND.

meaning, "Wake up and check on the weather." This became a daily ritual for me, and reporting to my father the condition of the weather became my first words of the day. My father was a quiet, witty, caring man whose words of encouragement created a sense of invitation. In hindsight, I know that my father got up with the light, kindled our wood stove in our one-room log home, and drank his first cup of coffee after he himself had gone outside to "check on the weather." I'm sure my father's enticement to check on the elements was also a discreet nudge to answer nature's call since our home had no plumbing.

The connection of the Yup'ik to the physical and spiritual worlds is affirmed through everyday activities among my people. Being born into a traditional Yup'ik-speaking household, and growing up speaking both my mother's Norton Sound Kotlik dialect and my father's general Central Yup'ik dialect, have given me insight about my own ties to the environment in which I live. If I had not had the opportunity to hear teachings about the survival of the Yup'ik people, and to have the support and encouragement of my parents and community members, I would not have had the privilege of becoming the educator I am today. I feel that my contribution to my people is to establish ties between the two worlds in which we live.

As traditional as my upbringing was, with the benefit of speaking and living my Yup'ik identity, it has given me the foundation today that has allowed me to prosper in the dominant Western culture. Had it not been for the connections I made to my

Connections

I feel that my contribution

to my people is to establish

ties between the two worlds

in which we live.

◄ Tununak resident Geraldine Fairbanks models a *kuspuk* (women's calico tunic) and *mukluks* (skin boots).

▼ Herring is woven into grass "garlands" to dry on outdoor racks. Here, Susie Angaiak collects the fish for storage.

surroundings during my childhood, I would not have been able to gain access and ownership to the outside world as an educator, a researcher, and a representative of my people in the area of education. It is humbling to have had the opportunity to pursue a college degree and teach at the university level. I attribute my success in this area to my childhood training, which taught me that all actions are related and that all have benefits and consequences.

I recall instances in which my growth as a Yup'ik person was constantly related to nature—our connection for survival—always through the knowledge of our elders, who carry on our traditions. During berry-picking season, and at times when we were on a hunting trip, the youngest was the one who would be told by the eldest in the camp to fetch water in the teakettle from the river. Upon fetching the water, the youngest would place the teakettle at the entryway of the tent in which we slept. If the youngest didn't fetch the water for the next morning, my parents would say, *Mer'irciqaakut,* meaning, "It will deplete us of water." In fear of not having any water to sustain us, I, being the youngest at most times, would fetch our water for the next morning without question.

In the old days, containers for keeping ample amounts of water were scarce. The elder family members expected the younger children to haul water for two reasons: first, to enlist the help of those most eager to please, and second, to pass along an awareness and appreciation of our dependence on the natural world. Without question, of course, we would do whatever was asked of us by our parents and other adults.

The daily life of the Yup'ik Eskimos has a close connection with nature— the provider of life, food, health, and future. Our Yup'ik language reflects this association. About half of Alaska's Yup'iks still speak the language, and its common use by the

◄ BASKET WEAVER MARYANN "ARNAUCUAQ" SUNDOWN IS AMONG THE ELDERS WHO ARE TEACHING THEIR CRAFT TO YOUNGER GENERATIONS.

▲ RACHEL SMART OF HOOPER BAY IS A RESPECTED WEAVER AND DOLL MAKER.

Respect for Life

The animals provided us with food to sustain us, and it is rightly so that we respected and continue to respect them.

▶ OSCAR RIVERS READIES TO JUMP TO AN ICE FLOE IN THE BERING SEA.

people of our region reveals its continuing relevance to everything pertaining to the survival of our people.

With or without a close tie to the Yup'ik language, our people continue to rely on our culture for their very existence. Subsistence hunting and gathering are major sources of food that the people in the Yup'ik region depend upon to live. Fish of

32

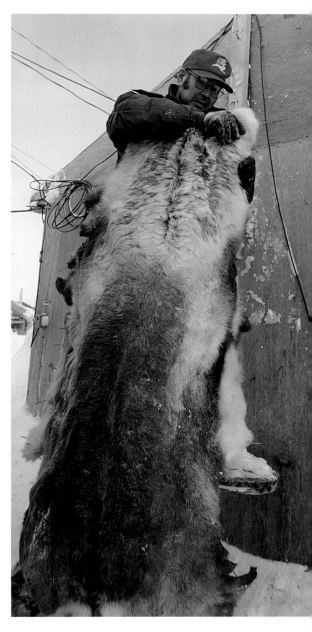

◄ VERONICA KAGANAK FLESHES A SEAL ON THE FLOOR OF HER UTILITY ROOM. VIRTUALLY NONE OF THE ANIMAL WILL BE WASTED.

▼ WESLEY HENRY REMOVES A FREEZE-DRIED CARIBOU HIDE THAT HUNG ON THE EXTERIOR WALL OF HIS HOUSE FOR THE WINTER.

different types year-round, moose, caribou, rabbit, ptarmigan, beaver, to name a few, are staples in the diet of people in the region. Wild foods provide physical and spiritual nourishment. For instance, I remember vividly how much respect we were taught to show to the animal carcasses. When my father came home with a rabbit, a fox, or a ptarmigan in the winter after a whole day's travel in the cold, he would set the animal

"Mer'irciqaakut"

*"It will deplete us of water,"
my parents would say. I would
fetch our water for the next
morning without question.*

► Spring sunshine edges over the frozen
Bering Sea near Scammon Bay.

Interconnections

From the time we awoke until the time we went to bed, there was some reflection on the interconnected natural world that continues to bring us life.

▲ James Gump of Hooper Bay uses marine mammal hide to make Yup'ik-style drums, which are struck from behind with a wooden wand.

▶▶ The fur of wolves and caribou adorn a Yup'ik girl's traditional headdress and dance fans.

▶▼ For Russian Orthodox believers Christmas arrives on January 7 in Lower Kalskag and other towns throughout Alaska.

in the entryway of our house. He then would caution us to make sure we didn't make any loud noises or run around wildly near the carcass. Before we could ask why, my parents would say that the spirit of the animal was "visiting" us to see whether we were capable of respect for it. After the visit, the spirit of the animal would return to its kind and report the condition of respect it had observed. If we were deferential during the animal's visit, we were assured by my parents that more food would enter our home.

Other ways of respecting animals that entered our home was to dress them expediently and put away the meat for meals. If it was a fox or a wolf, then my father would skin the animal and properly dispose of the carcass. After meals of fish or a seal in the summer, the younger children would take the bones of the fish or seal and reverently dispose of them into the water, saying, *Ataam taikina,* meaning, "Come back again," in hopes of more food from the ocean. Parents, other adults, and elders looked down upon any wasting of food. Being wasteful or disrespectful of food was a reminder that we might starve in the future.

The animals provided us with food to sustain us, and it is rightly so that we respected and continue to respect them. This continued connection with the elements and the animals is a concept that reminds us of how we survived in the harsh arctic climate, especially in those days before access to the conveniences of heating fuel, electricity, running water, and the like. From the time we awoke in the morning until the time we went to bed, there was some reflection on the interconnected natural world around us, the world that continues to bring us life.

Walkie Charles is a Yup'ik from Emmonak, a coastal village on the Yukon-Kuskokwim Delta in southwestern Alaska. He lives in Fairbanks and is on the faculty of the Alaska Native Language Center at the University of Alaska Fairbanks. Charles is a former visiting faculty at UAF School of Education and has a strong interest in literacy, language, and culture.

IÑUPIAT

Most Iñupiat people live along the harsh and treeless arctic coast, although a few villages are settled along big rivers between the coast and the Interior; some live as far inland as Anaktuvuk Pass, in the heart of the Brooks Range. Like the Siberian Yupik and Yup'ik, the people are Eskimo; yet the Iñupiaq language, lifestyle, and climate are more like those of the Canadian Inuit than of their fellow Alaskans.

Every year from November 18 through January 24, a period of sixty-seven days, there is no daylight in Barrow, the farthest-north ciy in the United States. Likewise, from May 10 to August 2, the northernmost Alaskans experience eighty-four days of continuous daylight. The people enjoy competing in ancient Native games, such as the One-Foot Kick, Ear Pull, or Knuckle Hop. Basketball and baseball are also popular sports.

The Iñupiat honor the seasons and special days with celebrations, such as the spring Whale Catch Festival, which thanks the whales that have given themselves to the people. The meat of marine mammals is essential to a healthy Iñupiat diet. Whaling crews must obey strict international laws as they try to catch migrating bowhead whales. Villagers along rivers rely on fish, moose, and caribou. For their subsistence lifestyle, traditional arts and crafts, games, dances, songs, language, and stories, the people depend on the generational knowledge and expertise handed down by the elders.

Honor Your Elders—
They Show You the Way in Life

RUTHIE LEE TATQAVIN RAMOTH-SAMPSON

In the Iñupiat region of northwest Alaska, the late Susie Anigniq Stocking of Kobuk once told the story of gathering willow bark for twisting into twine for fishnets. The people collected the willow bark in the early summer, walking

▲ HARRY BROWER AND OTHER WHALERS WEAR WHITE HUNTING PARKAS FOR CAMOUFLAGE; HE MADE THIS TRADITIONAL *UMIAK* (SKIN BOAT) USING BEARDED SEAL HIDE.

◄ A HUNTER WITH THE OLEMAUN CREW SCANS THE OPEN OCEAN FOR A PLUME OF VAPOR, SIGN OF AN EXHALING WHALE.

barefoot amid mosquitoes and thorny bushes. She said that they piled the willow strips high on their shoulders until you couldn't see a person's head anymore. Then they took the willow bark into their canoes. From then on, they kept the bark and twine damp as they fashioned it into nets or else it would crumble and there would be no fish to eat. She said they didn't realize how hard life was because it was "normal" for them.

Life in the Arctic can be harsh. If anyone survives many seasons, that individual deserves to be respected and honored. This is especially true of the Native elders of

Alaska. Just one hundred years ago, our ancestors lived completely off the land. They worked hard to survive, gathering wood and saving blubber for heat. They had no matches. They sewed all their fur and leather clothing by hand and moved seasonally to be at prime spots for harvesting food. Ingenuity, sheer will, and resourcefulness saved the Iñupiat in times of great hunger.

The late Alfred Taapsuk Stone of Noorvik spoke of how people survived famine. One time, a family ran out of food. The husband and wife began walking with their

▲ JUMBLED SEA AND SHORE ICE DWARFS A WHALING CAMP ALONG THE ARCTIC OCEAN NORTHWEST OF BARROW.

child to a cache of stored food. On the way, the husband died of starvation. His wife and child made it to the cache, but unfortunately, the mother ate too much after being famished for so long, and died soon after. The child was eventually rescued by a group of people passing through. This is one example of how our ancestors struggled to survive so we could live, and, consequently, our elders must be respected and honored simply for the fact that they survived such a hard life.

Elders are also the culture-bearers of so much wisdom and knowledge. Traditionally, they did not depend on the written word to remember anything; stories were passed from speaker ·to speaker, and therefore memory skills were keen. Whenever younger people were around, older people had the responsibility of giving them *algaqsruun* (advice). Such advice included being respectful of elders.

"Always help elders without expecting any pay." The Iñupiat said if you helped

▲ BLOCK AND TACKLE, MANPOWER, AND A SKIFF'S HORSEPOWER HELP TO LAND A BOWHEAD WHALE.

43

Showing the Way

The Iñupiat said if you helped

elders, you would live a long life.

► A BARROW MAN USES A HANDMADE FLESHING TOOL TO BEGIN THE BUTCHERING PROCESS.

▼ TRADITION DICTATES THAT THE FIRST SHARE OF WHALE MEAT IS IMMEDIATELY COOKED AND DISTRIBUTED TO THE CREW AND HELPERS. MALIGIAN HOPSON GETS TO WORK.

elders, you would live a long life. This was adhered to so closely that it included respecting anyone older than you. You had to obey your older siblings, aunts, uncles, older cousins, parents, and especially grandparents, without question. If they asked you to do an errand, you responded immediately. This was essential for cooperation so that everyone could work together to accomplish certain tasks, and in case of an emergency, lives could be saved.

Other nuggets of wisdom include such sayings as, *Nikaitchuatguuq piraqtut,* meaning, "Those who think they can, will accomplish something." Another translation is "Those who are confident actually get the job done," a phrase used to boost the confidence of anyone who was planning a seemingly impossible task. Such encouragement helped people learn to hunt giant whales and walrus, or sew elaborate clothing, or

dare to walk hundreds of miles to hunt caribou. When you make up your mind to do something, you can accomplish the task.

Another example of an Iñupiaq *algaqsruun* has to do with hospitality and sharing, which are often demonstrated by the elders. My uncle, Jonas Ramoth, originally of Selawik and now an elder in Kotzebue, recently related this saying: *Iuumguuq qanga mikiruq*. This translates as "It is said that a person's mouth is small," which encouraged people to be generous even if what they had to share appeared inadequate. It was enough to feed one mouth. My uncle also imparted this wisdom: *Isignaqtuq. Tupigguuq qaatlaitchuq.* This means "Come on inside. It is said that a house cannot burst." This was a way of saying that people are always welcome. We honor the traditional Iñupiat elders who heard these treasures of wise sayings and are still sharing them with anyone who is willing to listen.

When I was a little girl, I followed my grandmother, Dora Ballot, everywhere. I often visited the elderly couple who helped raise her, Richard and Fanny Jones. As we were growing up, we were taught to help them. We cut wood and carried it into the house. We chopped through the ice to haul water and did other simple chores for them. I remember pushing a small basket sled to take Fanny to church because, by that time, it was difficult for her to walk. Later, we walked Richard to church because he

▲ MEN FROM EUGENE BROWER'S WHALING CREW, IN WHITE HUNTING PARKAS, HELP TO REMOVE LARGE STRIPS OF *MUKTUK* (WHALE SKIN AND BLUBBER) FROM THE FIRST WHALE LANDED IN THE SPRING 2001 HUNT.

► KATHARINE CLEVELAND AND HER GRANDCHILDREN PICK WHITEFISH FROM THEIR NET ON THE KOBUK RIVER NEAR AMBLER.

▼ RICHARD EGNATY OF SLEETMUTE COMPETES IN THE ALASKA HIGH KICK AT THE ANNUAL WORLD ESKIMO-INDIAN OLYMPICS, HELD IN FAIRBANKS EACH SUMMER.

eventually became blind. They were usually kind enough to give us a piece of partially melted hard candy that they had saved from the Christmas distribution. In those days, that was a treat to work hard for. We did not help them just for a reward, however. Helping elders was a behavior that was taught to us and expected of us.

What an honor it is to help an elder. The elders are always thankful. They are very spiritual people and give thanks for being alive. They often express their appreciation with this blessing: "May you live a long life until you have gray hair like me." Even if they don't say it in so many words, you can see how thankful they are just by looking into their eyes.

All of the stories of fun times our elders had traveling all over the countryside are like precious stones one might gather. Elders love to get together to share funny stories, too. They lived through many changes, and their early cross-cultural experiences now inspire much humor. For instance, they enjoy telling about their first encounters with

"Nikaitchuatguuq piraqtut"

"Those who think they can,

will accomplish something."

Western food. They didn't know what pilot bread was, so they played Frisbee with it. They didn't know what flour was but they loved the flour-sack material. They dumped the flour on the ground and fashioned new garments with the cotton sacks. Another incident, about loose black tea, was recounted by my great-uncle, the late Elmer Ballot of Selawik, who was gracious in sharing much information with the younger generation. He told a story of a man named Ilaiq, who thought black tea tasted like old water from tundra ponds. Later, Ilaiq learned to love tea so strong that he refused to drink it if he could see the bottom of his cup.

Today, elders with traditional knowledge are becoming fewer and fewer in number. The treasured memories of all the things they did in their lifetimes are waiting to be told and shared. Our history is not written down in books; it is in the keen memories of our living elders. They know the tunes and lyrics to wonderful love songs. Many enjoy being out in the country and listening to the birds and catching fish to dry for

▲ KNOWN THROUGHOUT THE REGION FOR HER BASKETRY, MINNIE GRAY OF AMBLER SHAPES BIRCH BARK INTO BEAUTIFUL, FUNCTIONAL PIECES OF ART.

the winter. They know the place-names of camping spots, fishing areas, hunting grounds, and shortcuts on ancient trails. They have a healthy respect for the animals they harvest.

The elders also know words for concepts that many young people don't even think about. They know, for example, many terms for different types of snow. Hard-packed snow ideal for making emergency shelter is called *sikliq*. Snow that makes a crunching sound in cold weather is called *qikiggagnaq*. They used the prevailing winds to find out in which direction the grass had blown down or how snowdrifts had been shaped so that they could use them for navigation aids in a blizzard. Some may still remember the special names and stories for stars and constellations.

During their lifetimes, our elders walked hundreds of miles, dried and tanned hundreds of animal hides, picked thousands of berries, and processed fish and game through sheer hard work, just to make sure their children would survive. We give them tribute, for we are here today because of them. Indeed, we honor our elders for sharing *inuunialiq*, "the way of life."

◄ FAMILIES ON THE SEWARD PENINSULA HAVE BEEN HERDING REINDEER SINCE AS EARLY AS 1894. IN 1937, A FEDERAL ACT RESTRICTED REINDEER OWNERSHIP TO ALASKA NATIVES.

▲ ONE BY ONE, THE REINDEER ARE PINNED DOWN FOR DEHORNING AND INOCULATIONS. CLOSELY RELATED TO THE CARIBOU, MANY OF THESE FREE-RANGE ANIMALS RUN OFF WITH THEIR MIGRATING COUSINS EACH YEAR.

► LARRY DAVIS'S HERD IS BRIEFLY CORRALLED DURING SPRING ROUND-UP. HIS HOME AND REINDEER RANGE LIE WELL OUTSIDE THE CITY OF NOME ON THE SEWARD PENINSULA.

Ruthie Lee Tatqavin Ramoth-Sampson, daughter of Ralph and Emma Ramoth, is a Siilvingmiu Iñupiaq Eskimo from Selawik, Alaska. She now lives in Kotzebue and works as the Bilingual Education Coordinator for the Northwest Arctic Borough School District. Sampson is married to Luke and has four children and five grandchildren.

ALEUT

The Aleut people (or Unangan) settled along the rocky, windswept coasts of a thousand-mile island chain—the Aleutians—and on part of the Alaska Peninsula. A seafaring people, they thrived on the bounty of Alaska's waters. Women wove intricate baskets from the lush grasses that grow on the islands. Dancing, drumming, and singing were part of every celebration.

Russian fur traders arrived in the late 1700s and enslaved the Aleuts to hunt sea otters and fur seals. Thousands of people died through disease and war with the foreigners; the resource, too, was nearly decimated.

With the foreigners came Western beliefs and customs, and the people adopted the Russian Orthodox faith. One priest created an Aleut alphabet and translated the Bible; the people became literate and bilingual. In little more than two centuries, their traditional ways have melded into a unique Aleut-Russian culture.

When the United States purchased Alaska in 1867, Aleuts who were laboring for the Russian fur traders continued their work for a new government; officials controlled the Natives' every decision, even in personal matters. During World War II, the U.S. government evacuated the Aleuts from their villages to camps in Southeast Alaska. Some villages were never repopulated. In 1975, Aleuts sued the federal goverment for nearly a century of virtual enslavement. Reparations were received in 1988.

Accept What Life Brings— You Cannot Control Many Things

◆

PHILIP KELLY

◉

I am Philip Kelly, the son of Migley Kelly, the last Traditional

Chief of Egegik. He was born in 1919; I was born in 1944.

Egegik is located at the mouth of the Egegik River on

the Alaska Peninsula, the farthest-north Aleut village on the

▲ AN ATKA ISLAND DANCER PREPARES TO PERFORM AT THE ALASKA
FEDERATION OF NATIVES CONVENTION.

◄ UNALASKA'S HOLY ASCENSION OF CHRIST CHURCH FACES EAST, AS
RUSSIAN ORTHODOX TRADITION PRESCRIBES.

▲ SUBSISTENCE FISHERMEN AND
BROTHERS, MOSES (LEFT) AND LARRY
DIRKS USE MORE MODERN METHODS
THAN THEIR ANCESTORS, YET STILL RELY
ON THE SEA TO FEED THEIR FAMILIES.

the peninsula. Our people have had a long history in a demanding environment, and our survival depended upon accepting what we could not change.

To the north of our village by about forty miles is Naknek, considered a Yup'ik Eskimo community in Yup'ik territory. The old ones in the village told stories of tribal border wars that raged between the two villages. When an Aleut hunter wandered too far north into Yup'ik hunting grounds and did not return, a search party would sally forth, not to return until the hunter was found, usually dead and mutilated. His entrails would be strung over the alder bushes near where his body lay. The search party would mark the spot where the Aleut hunter was slain. In retaliation, our tribe marked the southern bounds of Yup'ik hunting grounds in the same manner. Tribal conflicts continued to be a part of Aleut life until another race of people came to Egegik. These men came from a place far across the water, toward the setting sun—a place called Russia.

Our people did not fare well when the Russians came searching for furs. The Russians took our young hunters and pressed them into service, never returning them. The Russians would keep them until they died. Because the Russians treated the Aleuts so badly, the tribes of Egegik and Ugashik declared war on them. A Russian convoy of canoes and skin boats on its way to Kodiak was ambushed at a place called the Small Narrows at the eastern end of Becharof Lake. It is said that five hundred Aleuts attacked the convoy and only two Russians escaped the carnage and made their way to Kanatak, the community on the Pacific side of the Alaska Peninsula.

Survival

Our people did not fare well when the Russians came searching for furs.

◄ PAT LEKANOFF-GREGORY CREATES BENTWOOD VISORS IN THE SAME SHAPE THAT HER PEOPLE HAVE USED FOR CENTURIES. OLD-TIME BENTWOOD VISORS WERE OFTEN DECORATED WITH SEA LION WHISKERS AND FEATHERS.

► DANCERS IN TRADITIONAL DRESS PERFORM FOR THE PUBLIC AT QUYANA ALASKA, A MULTICULTURAL CELEBRATION HELD EACH YEAR AS PART OF THE ALASKA FEDERATION OF NATIVES CONVENTION. QUYANA MEANS "THANK YOU" IN THE YUP'IK LANGUAGE.

▼ LEKANOFF-GREGORY SHOWS OFF HER HANDIWORK.

Eventually, we became used to the Russians. They introduced our people to their Russian Orthodox religion, which is still evident to this day and played a major role in uniting the people in the village. For instance, caroling and feasts involved the entire community during Christmas and Easter celebrations. Still, when I weigh the benefits of the church against the cruelties inflicted upon the Aleuts after first contact with the Russians, I do not know if the scales balance even now.

The Russians' arrival heralded changes in the Aleut way of life. Then came the Americans. Fish canneries came to Egegik around the early 1900s. The change was for the better, however, as the fishing industry provided jobs in the canneries and handling fishing boats. There was a Libby, McNeil and Libby plant across the river from the village and an Alaska Packers Association cannery in Egegik. Later came the Egegik Packing Company. Most of the Aleut men were employed as captains of company-owned, thirty-two-foot sailboats. The price of salmon in 1934, according to

▲ HOME FOR ALEUT LEADER LARRY
MERCULIEFF IS SAINT PAUL ISLAND, THE
BREEDING GROUNDS FOR FUR SEALS.

my uncle, Nick Abalama, was ten cents per fish. Our people fished in the summer for
the canneries, making enough money to buy the dry goods needed to survive the
winter. The rest of the summer season was spent catching and drying fish for our dog

teams. We used the teams in winter to run our traplines, catching fur for clothing and
to sell. The land fed us with caribou, moose, seals, ducks, geese, and ptarmigan.
Contentment was a warm house, food, a dog team, traps, and bullets.

► FEDERAL FUNDING FOR HISTORIC SITES HAS HELPED PRESERVE THE HOLY ASCENSION OF CHRIST CHURCH AND ITS VALUABLE ICONS.

▼ THE WATERS SURROUNDING AND RUNNING THROUGH THE ALEUTIANS ARE RICH IN SEAFOOD THAT HAS SUPPORTED THE FIRST PEOPLE FOR THOUSANDS OF YEARS.

The only time fresh food ever made its way to Egegik in those days was when the steamship made its twice-yearly visit: once in the spring and again in the fall about a month before freeze-up. The Alaska Steamship Line would bring summer supplies and workers for the three canneries that operated in the Egegik River. The steamship brought new experiences to Egegik, like eating real apples and oranges, which we had read about in books at the schoolhouse but had never tasted before. We enjoyed many new things, but we took them in stride.

The outside world intruded on the Aleut people in a major way during World War II. Japanese forces bombed Unalaska Island on June 3, 1942, and again on June 5. That day, too, they invaded Kiska Island, where they took ten prisoners of war, and Attu Island, on the western end of the Aleutian Islands. About forty Attu villagers were taken to a POW camp in Japan, where conditions were horrible, and disease and squalor claimed the lives of another sixteen people. Saying that they were protecting other Aleuts from the enemy, the U.S. government evacuated 881 villagers from the treeless Aleutian Chain and Pribilof Islands to primitive camps in the rain forest of Southeast Alaska. In many ways, conditions were as bad as those of a POW camp. Few of the very old, the infirm, or the very young made it through those years. We Egegik Aleuts on the mainland Alaska Peninsula were relatively isolated from those troubles, and none of our people were evacuated. When I was a boy, however, I heard about a Japanese spy who had been mapping channels in our region. He was arrested at one of our canneries. Although Egegik's everyday life seemed to go on without disruption, we Aleuts knew that our world had changed yet again.

"Survival is the ability to adapt to any situation one encounters!" Those words of advice were drilled in my mind at an early age, and the lessons kept coming. In the late 1950s, when I was an eighteen-year-old commercial fishing captain, I put my boat and partner in a dire situation one morning floating on the high tide at the mouth of Frank's Creek in the Egegik Fishing District. My cousin, Jack Abalama, and I had just caught a load of red salmon that left the back end of our boat floating just two feet above the water. That meant that a wave only three feet high could wash over our stern and sink us. Our bottom bumped on the hard-packed sand as we tried to find our way out of the creek's mouth. We had to get to deep water, drop our anchor, and clean the nets so the

fish weight would be distributed evenly in the fish bins. Boats around us were getting stuck. In the excitement I could not remember exactly how we came in through the shallow channel. Another ten minutes and it would make no difference; the tide was going out fast and we would be high and dry with 1,200 fish onboard. This was not good. In no time, the incoming tide and wave action would lift and slam the three-and-a-half-ton boat with the extra weight of the fish and knock the caulking out of the wooden seams. The bilge pumps would not be able to pump all the water out. The boat would sink before it could float! It had happened to other boats. The crew of one boat made it to shore, a half-mile away, but another had lost a man in the pounding, cold, gray water. Jack flashed a worried look at me and then went back to trying to find a way out.

Looking at the water's surface could tell you where deep water was. Our ability to read water was no help in this situation, however, because the water was shallow all over. Some seals were already sunning themselves on the sandbars that were beginning to show. Seals! If frightened, they would head for deep water! I steered our boat directly for the sandbar and the seals and had Jack shoot the rifle in the air above the animals. The seals scrambled, and I managed to follow their bobbing black heads out into deep water and the channel. We were saved by a herd of seals, animals that generally were not liked because they ate the fish in our nets. I never bothered seals after that.

We Aleuts have adjusted to life in many ways, surviving by bending with the winds of time. One cannot control many things.

▲ Unalaskan artist Gertrude Svarny creates sought-after carvings, bentwood hats, and baskets.

Philip Kelly holds a bachelor's degree in speech with a minor in creative writing from the University of Alaska Fairbanks. While attending UAF, he represented Alaska Native students at the October 1966 meeting that established the Alaska Federation of Natives. He has worked in the Matanuska-Susitna Borough School District for ten years and is now a bilingual tutor/advisor at Houston Junior/Senior High School. He is retired from commercial fishing after thirty years in the business and makes his home in Wasilla, but he still has ties to Egegik.

TLINGIT

The Tlingit people are the dominant Native group of Southeast Alaska, in number and in size of their traditional homeland. They claim most of the Alaska Panhandle—a far-reaching mass of mountains, islands, waterways, and forest—as well as a good portion of inland Canada. Their culture evolved in close relationship with the sea, in the lushness and abundance of a rain forest. Robes, button blankets, drums, totems, masks, and jewelry bear unique clan symbols, and clan membership is passed from mother to child in an ancient tradition that has carried forward into contemporary times. Practices and rules surrounding potlatches are also time-honored and revered.

The Tlingit fiercely defended their homeland in the early 1800s, but Russian firepower overwhelmed them. The city of New Archangel (now Sitka) was the capital of Russian America. In the late 1800s, Tlingit clans continued to control the trading routes linking the coastal people to those inland. Gold Rush stampeders paid Native packers to move their supplies over high mountain passes to reach the Klondike goldfields. The Tlingit were eventually overcome by foreigners, and their traditional ways were oppressed until the late twentieth century, when a cultural revival began to build.

Some ten thousand Tlingit live in Alaska today, about five hundred of whom speak their Native language. Neighboring Tsimshian and Haida people live in small pockets at the southernmost tip of the Panhandle.

Have Patience—Some Things Cannot Be Rushed

NORA MARKS DAUENHAUER

My mother, Emma, sits at the wheel of a twenty-five-foot fishing boat named *Nora*. Behind her, giant breakers roll in from the North Pacific. They lift her boat and lower it. They lift her, she imagines, as high as the mast, and drop her down

▲ JON ROWAN, TOTEM POLE CARVER AND SCHOOLTEACHER, IS HELPING TO INSTILL CULTURAL PRIDE IN HIS TLINGIT STUDENTS.

◄ SUBSISTENCE FISHERMEN FROM THE VILLAGE OF KLAWOCK BALANCE PRECARIOUSLY AS THEY HAUL IN A NETFUL OF SALMON.

again. There is a breeze on the ocean, making the water black, breaking the silvery surface. Half circling her and the boat are islands, reefs, and rocks. Some she can't see; others she can. The giant breakers smash themselves against the reefs, rocks, and kelp. She awaits a signal from the beach, from my father, who has gone seal hunting on the other side of the island. She feels like she's turning to stone from trying to be patient and keep calm. Her five small children are in the boat with her.

This was not the first time she was alone on a boat, waiting for her husband to return. In all her married life she probably did more waiting with her children on a boat than on land. The Tlingit homeland is along the Southeast Alaska archipelago, in the largest temperate rain forest in the world, and our culture is oriented to the forest, beach, and sea. Like most Tlingit fishermen, my father also loved to hunt and trap, and this was part of our family's subsistence. But anchoring the boat offshore from some hunting grounds wasn't possible, so my mother had to keep the boat moving. My

◄ TLINGIT CARVER NATHAN JACKSON AT HIS STUDIO IN SAXMAN.

▲ JACKSON'S WORK IS COVETED AMONG COLLECTORS AND MUSEUMS.

Culture

Robes, button blankets, drums,

totems, masks, and jewelry

bear unique clan symbols.

▲ JOE HOTCH OF KLUKWAN'S EAGLE MOIETY DONS FULL TRADITIONAL REGALIA. THE KILLER WHALE HAT IN HIS HANDS WAS CARVED MORE THAN A CENTURY AGO.

►▲ BOLD COLOR, CLAN SYMBOLS, AND DETAILED BUTTON WORK ARE HALLMARKS OF TLINGIT ROBES.

►▼ TLINGIT DANCER ERNIE BERNHARDT.

father taught her how to handle the boat so that when he went ashore she could take over. Many times she took the wheel when my father was trolling for salmon. She knew the salmon fishing areas well, but she was nervous about the breakers. In places like this, where no anchor would hold, she had to idle the engine, move back and forth in place, not really go anywhere, but keep the boat off the rocks.

My mother was born near the mouth of the Alsek River, but she had never skippered a boat in her childhood there. After marrying my father in her teens, she accompanied him as a helper on their little boat, the *Nora*. The ocean-going power-boats were different from the river seiners at Alsek, but she caught on quickly. She learned how to read the water and how to make the right move at the right time.

▲ ALBERT PADDY OF KLUKWAN MOTORS
OUT TO CHECK HIS SUBSISTENCE NETS ON
THE CHILKAT RIVER.

I see my mother at the wheel again, this time on the *New Anny*, the family fishing boat I grew up on, approaching South Pass, heading seaward against the incoming tide. This time, my father is sick and unable to pilot, and my mother has to navigate. My teenaged cousin, Betty, is beside her. South Rock, a huge rock, is to her left. If the tide catches them, the boat will end up on the rock.

The entrance to Icy Strait from the outer coast and North Pacific is a choice of two ways around Inian Islands, called North Pass and South Pass. South Pass, between Inian Islands and the tip of Chichagof Island, is feared and respected because of the strong tides. "It's a wicked place," my brother has told me. "The tide makes it wicked." To take a boat through, the captain must know the behavior of the tide. If it is coming in, you have to buck the current. It takes longer to go through during a tide change, and it's difficult to keep the boat off the rocks when the tide is knocking you around. Sometimes you can wait out the tide change, but in this case there is no safe place; so she has to take her only chance and go. She knows family members have died in these waters. Her husband's aunts started off from a bay nearby after picking berries, and the tide turned on them. They never made it home to Hoonah. No sign of them or their canoes was ever found.

White-knuckled, my mother steers the boat through the churning sea, breakers smashing on the rocks and draining off them in froth. Approaching the pass, she throttles the engine as much as she dares. You can't go too fast and you can't go too slow. She can see the cauldrons of boiling tide pools. She can see the bottom of the sea

churning up in giant pillows beside the boat. She can see the tide coming toward her, looking at times like a dark and rolling hill, one side calm and the other side jumping with breakers. Later, at Elfin Cove, the *New Anny* draws up to the float. Shy and still shaking from going through South Pass, my mother parks the boat and ties up without any trouble, despite the distraction of casual spectators on the dock.

My mother's patience was called upon as a boat skipper, but also in other tasks related to providing for the family, such as berry picking. She never stops talking about her homeland on the Alsek River and her father's homeland on the Italio River, and the berries they picked there. When her in-laws were alive, she went on berry-picking expeditions with them. While my father was alive, she went with him and his crew to pick berries. When they grew infirm and passed away, she went with friends. In the gathering of berries, there were times of plenty and times of slim pickings. The fondest family memories are of the times of plenty. My paternal grandmother described one bay where strawberries were as abundant as "a place where a red blanket was thrown down." They picked the berries as fast as they could, filling can after can, limited only by the speed of their fingers. At times the berries were described "as if they were glowing through the leaves." Salmonberries were so ripe that each was like a yarn hat. Blueberries were so ripe and plentiful that the branches lay on the ground "as if they were tired" and had to be lifted to be picked.

Such memories are a berry picker's enduring hope and dream, but in most seasons berries were harder to find, and their harvest took more patience. Maybe each trip

▲ THE CHILKAT RIVER WENDS THROUGH THE NORTHERN REACHES OF THE SOUTHEAST PANHANDLE.

would yield just one or two jars of berries for the winter. But my mother enjoyed every minute of berry picking, during times of plenty as well as times of lean. She loved to see the fruits of her labor in jars, and she took pleasure in giving them to friends.

My mother loved to dry fish in her smokehouse. She smoked the halibut and salmon my father and brothers brought in so that the family could enjoy the fish all winter. To make delicious dryfish takes a lot of patience and care. You must keep the fire small enough so that the fish don't cook. On the other hand, the fire must be hot enough so that the fish don't spoil. The goal is nice, flaky salmon that breaks at a slight touch and can be chewed with ease—not jaw-breakingly dry.

Occasionally, my mother had some of the men from her church bring her fish to dry for fund-raising dinners. Everyone who tasted her salmon loved it, and she loved to share it with family and friends. I agree: she did make the best-tasting dryfish! In fact, her family savored it so much that she sometimes had to hide her stash. When her granddaughters discovered her dryfish and got into it, they would eat it all up, if possible.

The great patience with which my mother did everything paid off in ways too numerous to mention here, in the many blessings she receives today from young and old. I guess you could say that her family was her driving force. She did everything for us.

It was easy to accept this writing assignment; it was harder to get started, taking a bit of—yes—patience. Words began to flow when I decided to write about my mom. Patience is not just a concept. All of my ideas and examples came from childhood images of my mother, as she embodied them. She's the most patient person I know. As I complete this essay, our extended family and friends are gathering to celebrate her eighty-eighth birthday.

◄ TLINGIT TOTEMS ARE A COMMON SIGHT IN SOUTHEAST, ON PUBLIC AND PRIVATE LANDS AS WELL AS IN MUSEUMS. THIS STORY POLE WAS ERECTED AT TOTEM BIGHT STATE PARK.

◄▲ A HUNGRY BLACK BEAR PULLS A FISH FROM ANAN CREEK.

▲ BALD EAGLES CONGREGATE ALONG THE CHILKAT RIVER BY THE THOUSANDS EVERY FALL.

Nora Marks Dauenhauer was born in Juneau, Alaska, and was raised in Juneau and Hoonah, as well as on the family fishing boat and in seasonal subsistence sites around Icy Strait, Glacier Bay, and Cape Spencer. Her creative and expository writing has been widely published and anthologized, and she has received many honors and awards. With her husband, Richard, Dauenhauer also works on Tlingit language and folklore publications. She has four children, twelve grandchildren, and five great-grandchildren.

A L U T I I Q

The Alutiiq people of the Kodiak Archipelago, Alaska Peninsula, and Kenai Peninsula are related by language to the Yup'ik Eskimos, but for years they have been misidentified as Aleuts. Many lifestyle similarities exist, but the Alutiiq are a unique people with their own body of human history, stories, dances, and songs.

Like the Aleuts, the Alutiiq were traditionally a coastal people who depended on the sea for their survival, hunting sea mammals from skin-covered kayaks. Raincoats were fashioned from sewing together strips of seal gut, a naturally waterproof element. And depending on the availability of wood, homes were built in the most heat-efficient way, partially underground.

Also like the Aleuts, the Alutiiq ancestors warred against Russian arrivals who enslaved the people to assist with hunting fur seals and sea otters. During the Russian-American Company's most powerful years of fur trading, the city of Kodiak on Kodiak Island was the company headquarters and capital of the colony. Through the years, Alutiiq culture blended with Russian culture. Today many Alutiiq people are members of the Russian Orthodox Church and bear Russian surnames.

Throughout the region, findings from archaeological sites are helping the Alutiiq people regain some of their lost identity. Of the estimated three thousand Alutiiq people, about four hundred still speak the language. Two dialects within the Alutiiq language are Koniag and Chugach.

Pray for Guidance—
Many Things Are Not Known

♦

SVEN HAAKANSON JR.

◉

Stories have been passed down through generations of the Alutiiq people about how our shamans foretold of a religion coming from the West that we should embrace, leaving our traditional beliefs behind. When Russian Orthodox priests

▲ STELLA ZEEDER HARVESTS SEA URCHINS AT LOW TIDE.

◀ ELDER S. ZEEDER SR. OF KODIAK OFTEN VISITS HIS BOYHOOD HOME IN AKHIOK.

▲ LIVING OFF THE ROAD SYSTEM,
VILLAGERS COMMONLY USE ALL-TERRAIN
VEHICLES TO GET AROUND TOWN.

► AN ALUTIIQ CHILD IS ENGROSSED BY
THE BEAUTY OF A FLOWER BUD.

first arrived on Kodiak Island in 1794, Alexander Baranov, the director of the Russian-American Company, restricted them from baptizing the Native people. But once the priests broke free of his reign and traveled to all of the villages, our people greeted them at the beach, embracing the Russian Orthodox religion without coercion or any form of bribery. Today each village maintains an Orthodox church and a strong belief in what it symbolizes. Though currently skeptical about organized religion, I was brought up as an Orthodox follower, and I learned the power of prayer; in the face of the unknown, we cannot expect answers, but we can ask for guidance. I believe this spirituality, originating in traditional beliefs and continuing through orthodoxy, runs strong in the Alutiiq.

As I reflect upon my spiritual and cultural pilgrimage, I realize that this idea of acknowledging the unknown and embracing it has been apparent in my life and in the lives of my people. What caused an entire culture to change faiths, yet to retain dignity and identity? Why our shamans chose to relinquish their power is something we will never know or understand. As a result of recent archaeology and scholarship, however, there are a few things we can know.

Growing up on Kodiak Island, we never gave much thought to our heritage, and in fact it was never discussed at home or in school. We called ourselves Aleuts and never thought any differently until the early 1990s. Today we are called Alutiiq, and we call ourselves Sugpiat, translated as "the real people."

Through my years of college and graduate school, the depth of my knowledge about our heritage and understanding of its importance has come from many sources: my parents, elders across the island, and spiritual and academic scholars. Each one has guided my journey.

Master Mariners

The Alutiiq were traditionally a coastal people who depended on the sea for their survival, hunting sea mammals from skin-covered kayaks.

◄ LIKE MEN IN VILLAGES ALL ACROSS ALASKA, EPHRAIM AGNOT JR. OF AKHIOK IS A FISHERMAN, CARPENTER, AND JACK-OF-ALL-TRADES.

Sugpiat

Today we are called Alutiiq, and we call ourselves Sugpiat, translated as "the real people."

The Sugpiat, once a strong nation of more than twenty thousand people, were overtaken by the Russians in 1784. When we lost control of our land, we lost control of our destiny and our traditional way of living, yet our spirits were not broken. The true story has only begun to unfold in the last two decades, for the Sugpiat and for myself. I started research into my heritage and history to learn about who we are as an indigenous people. My journey has taken me down a very dark road. To learn how my people managed to survive cultural genocide, humiliation, and more over the past two centuries of European rule has saddened my soul but strengthened my spirit of resolve to make a difference.

Back in 1784, the Sugpiat of Kodiak were subjugated by the Russians at a place called Refuge Rock. The Alutiiq named it *Awa'uq* (a-WOW-uk), which means "to be numb." The site of Awa'uq went unknown until it was rediscovered in August 1991 by an archaeological team of which I was a member. We were unprepared for the impact this historic place would have on the Sugpiat; its discovery brought to light a tragic history and painful memories.

Historical accounts tell us that the explorer Grigori Ivanovich Shelikov arrived on Kodiak Island with three ships that had set sail in 1783 from Okhotsk, Russia. Within a month of their arrival, they subdued the Native people and established a fort in Three Saints Bay. Shelikov, known as the founder of Russian America, brought to Kodiak an Alutiiq slave named Kuspuk from the Aleutian Islands. He served as his translator and informant, helping Shelikov locate and conquer the islanders who had until this point kept the Russians off Kodiak Island. On the morning of August 13, Shelikov and his men attacked Awa'uq, taking women and children as hostages and killing those who resisted. This tragic story was forgotten until our archaeological team rediscovered it in 1991.

◄▲ VILLAGE OF AKHIOK.

◄ THREE-YEAR-OLD TIM D. MELOVEDOFF JR. PLAYS ALONG TIDE POOLS.

▲ PHYLLIS PETERSON'S SURNAME, LIKE AUTHOR SVEN HAAKANSON'S, OFFERS CLUES ABOUT SCANDINAVIAN IMMIGRATION AND INTERMARRIAGE AMONG THE ALUTIIQ PEOPLE.

Russian influence

When an outsider visits one of our villages, it appears that little remains of our traditional heritage.

When we climbed the rock for the first time, fog surrounded the island and an uneasy feeling of being watched came over me. While I brushed off my uneasiness as a product of bad weather, a sense of loss filled my mind. This was the site where my people lost hundreds of lives and lost control of their own land and people to outsiders. We ended up spending half the night on the island and were eventually picked up by my uncle. A year later, we returned to excavate the site and uncovered the story about the losses suffered by the Sugpiat. While it wasn't a large battle at the rock, the loss of life was one-sided. Although the Russians didn't lose a single life, the Sugpiat lost five hundred or more. Many were said to have thrown themselves off the cliffs. This was only the beginning of the tragedy. Over the next ten years, Grigori Shelikov and his successor, Alexander Baranov, enslaved the Sugpiat. History books have made heroes out of these men; only recently have we been able to shine a light on their true characters and the way they treated the Native people.

Shelikov stated in his accounts that there were more than 50,000 people on the island and that 5,000 individuals were involved in the battle. While we can naturally assume such numbers were an exaggeration by Shelikov, the point about such a large population at initial contact shows how many people died in a very short time. The Sugpiat population was less than 7,000 by 1794, and by 1867, a solid census tallied just 1,943 individuals. If I deflate Shelikov's original tally and estimate that there were just 10,000 Sugpiat on the island when the Russians arrived, that means 80 percent of the population was wiped out in the eighty years between first contact and the census of 1867; most of the losses occurred in the first two decades. By today's standards, this would be considered genocide, yet the Sugpiat continue to exist. How could this be, and what gives us the strength to survive?

When an outsider visits one of our villages, it appears that little remains of our traditional heritage because we speak English and live in modern houses. As we learn more about our past, however, we have come to respect and embrace our heritage, which has kept our culture alive and continues to guide us. The turning point in my own awareness about the importance of understanding our past came in 1988, when I attended the Sixth Annual Inuit Studies Conference in Copenhagen, Denmark. I listened to a lecture about the Aleut people given by Dr. Lydia Black, a well-known Alaska anthropologist and Russian-American historian. By the end of her presentation, I realized that I knew very little about my own cultural birthright. I had to ask myself why I was on the other side of the world learning about our history. I decided then that I should be home learning about Sugpiat culture. I was not alone in this realization, because at the same time other Sugpiat on Kodiak were becoming aware of the importance of learning about our past.

We are on a journey, and we pray for guidance because we can never know what to expect or where we will end up. As we learn and understand more about our past, we can use our heritage to guide our path as we explore an unknown future.

► LITTLE STEPHANIE BRENTESEN IS AN ATTENTIVE OBSERVER AT THE WEDDING OF HER MOTHER, PHYLLIS AMODO.

Sven Haakanson Jr. holds a doctorate in anthropology from Harvard University. He is the executive director of the Alutiiq Museum and Archaeological Repository in the city of Kodiak on Kodiak Island. He works closely with the Alutiiq Heritage Foundation Board and museum staff in guiding the direction of the Alutiiq Museum. Haakanson lives in Kodiak with his wife, Balika.

T S I M S H I A N

The Tsimshian people of Alaska live in the community of Metlakatla on Annette Island, near the southern tip of the Southeast panhandle. They are relatively recent transplants, with ancestral roots in or near the coast of northern British Columbia, Canada. In 1857, William Duncan, an Anglican lay missionary, settled among the Tsimshian in Canada. Thirty years later, Duncan led 823 Tsimshian from "Old" Metlakatla in Canada to resettle on Alaska's Annette Island, at a place they first called New Metlakatla. There, Duncan created a Victorian-style community in the wilderness and strictly controlled his flock, replacing Native cultural expression with economic activities he thought would allow the people to compete in the modern world.

Although much of Tsimshian culture was lost in the move to Metlakatla, the people maintain ties with relatives in Canada, and a number of contemporary Tsimshian are working to restore their traditions, such as potlatching, dancing, language, and art.

The Tsimshian of Alaska now number about thirteen hundred individuals who depend on the sea and forest for their subsistence, inspiration, and livelihood. And, like the Tlingit and Haida, these Tsimshian are known again for their striking regalia, carved totems, panels, and other art forms that are based on bird or animal symbols that represent their clans and subclans.

Live Carefully—What You Do Will Come Back to You

◆

David Boxley

◉

It is as old as our people, the thought that your actions, good

or bad, will come back to visit you. Growing up in the village,

I saw early on that you got a label, a view others had of you

by your response to various things, even if your intentions

▲ Iris Huckleberry picks greens and berries during an outing with baby Jacklynn.

◄ Annette Island is one of the warmest, rainiest places in the state.

▲ COMMERCIAL FISHERMAN WALT WARREN
WORKS HARD AND LONG ABOARD THE *BONNIE*
DURING THE FISHING AND SHRIMPING SEASONS.

were something totally different from what was interpreted. A reputation can be a bonus or a hindrance, especially if you want to be taken seriously at some point. Some miscue or youthful indiscretion may stand between you and the respect you feel you've earned, even as you move into the role of "elder." Your choices may affect not only you, but the generations that follow.

I come from a unique, history-filled village—Metlakatla—as a result of decisions made by my ancestors. They chose not just to move from Old Metlakatla in 1887, but thirty years earlier, they decided to listen to William Duncan, an Englishman who said he carried the word of God in a book. The choices those Tsimshian people made to leave behind their Native ways created, changed, and directed the history of our people to where it is today.

Some of us are trying to recover what was lost through that move. Although not alone in this cultural revival, I find I have contributed significantly to a "reaching back" to gather what can still be salvaged of our potlatch culture, which was left behind abruptly in order to "progress" and be successful in the New World—one that was not of our choosing or under our control.

Metlakatla

In 1857, Duncan led 823 Tsimshian from "Old" Metlakatla in Canada to resettle on Alaska's Annette Island, at a place they first called New Metlakatla.

▲ GORDON RIDLEY PROCESSES SALMON AT THE CANNERY IN METLAKATLA.

Because of the choices my great-grandparents made to leave the old ways behind, I grew up in a community that did not really know what was missing. Well, maybe there was an inkling—the language, fishing, subsistence, and this vague realization that somehow we were special, a special people with a unique history. Beyond the missionary's influence, there remained glimmers of the fabulous culture that the Tsimshian had developed over millennia.

A potlatch is a feast that also involves dancing and the exchange of gifts. When our people potlatched, they made significant impressions on the minds and hearts of those who witnessed their endeavors. The visitor knew that the vast food outlay and the amount of gift giving and time spent were an investment, not impoverishing, or time-wasting, as some white observers surmised. Good hosts later became guests, and the "gifts" they gave came back in significant and increased amounts. Still, in 1885, British Columbia outlawed potlatching, and it remained outlawed until the 1950s. The reciprocal exchange system in potlatching that was the hub of the Tsimshian cultural wheel was disrupted, and some Native people went to jail for dancing and giving gifts.

▲ ADORNED IN TIMELESS REGALIA,
PAUL BRENDIBLE LEADS THE DANCERS.

▶ THE KILLER WHALE CLAN DANCES
AT THE FOUR CLANS LONGHOUSE.

I gave the first-ever potlatch in Metlakatla in 1982 to honor my grandparents. There have been many since then, but that one started it all.

In 1996–97, I was involved with putting on the first-ever Tsimshian potlatch-type event for the Alaska Native community in Seattle. The idea that you could come to a cultural event and be fed for free, pay no admission price, be an important part of the proceedings as a witness, and be entertained was well received. Those who attended clamored for us to do it again, and the next year, we did.

My dance group, the Tsimshian Haayuuk, grew out of those celebrations. People came to the group excited and hungry to celebrate the culture they had only heard about. The journey since has been eventful and not without trials, but those who persevered know they are a part of something that has changed life for all of us. I am particularly stirred by the little ones, the three- and four-year-olds like Jerome Nathan and Harald Hyllseth, who were born during the group's formation. They know no other way except to gather every Tuesday to sing and dance to the beat of the box drum, and to perform in handmade button robes in front of the world with no timidity or fear. That's a payday, a "come back to you," if anything could be. I love that.

As an artist, I am fortunate to be making a living doing something I love. I'm also very aware of the responsibility I have to share knowledge of our traditions. To be a culture-bearer means that if I do not pass on what I know, the culture will die with me. Passing our culture on to other Native people is how I help it stay alive. On a Tuesday night, when little Jerome Nathan watches and emulates his father, Ben, by dancing the wolf dance (celebrating his father's clan's connection to the wolf), I see a day when he passes it to another. And the culture lives.

◄ CULTURAL EXPRESSION IN DRESS, SONG, STORYTELLING, LANGUAGE, ART, AND POTLATCHING IS ONCE AGAIN PART OF EVERYDAY LIFE FOR ALASKA'S TSIMSHIAN PEOPLE. FROM LEFT ARE CARLA SCHLEUSNER, CHRIS LEASK, AND MELODY LEASK IN THEIR DANCE FINERY.

▲ SIX-YEAR-OLD VAN LEWIS SCRAMBLES OVER A STATUE THAT WAS ERECTED NEAR THE METLAKATLA HARBOR.

▲ JACK AND IRIS HUCKLEBERRY ARE
THE PROUD PARENTS OF ONE-YEAR-
OLD JACKLYNN, WHO WILL GROW UP
KNOWING HER CULTURAL HERITAGE.

► THE FOUR CLANS TOTEM POLE
IN METLAKATLA WAS CARVED BY
DAVID BOXLEY.

I think taking care what you say and whom you say it to is a standard to aspire to. My grandfather said to me, "Talk nice to the people and they gonna talk nice to you." We know that some people within the Native world speak unkindly of other Native peoples. It comes from places outsiders may or may not understand. The story of two crab fishermen applies here. There were two crab fishermen: one Indian, one white. The white man couldn't keep his crabs from escaping from his barrel. He saw that the Indian's crabs never got out of his barrel, so he asked, "How do you do it?" The Indian answered, "Every time one of my crabs tries to crawl out, the others pull him back down."

There are different ways to look at the subject I am writing about. The one that I'd like to emphasize is living as if you are aware that we all affect everyone else around us. Our triumphs and failures as humans are not just limited to our own private space, but we touch other people. Even down the road, the foundation we lay is built upon by our descendants.

One of the things that I am very aware of is the disdain modern Native people have for those who call excessive attention to themselves or are seen as "acting better than us." Even when you might not have that in mind yourself, a generation of hardships and anti-Indian sentiment seems to have put us into the "try to achieve success, it helps us all, but don't succeed because it makes me look like a failure" kind of outlook. When I was trying to help bring our culture and the pride in its knowledge back to my village, I ran headfirst into that wall many times. Like I said, any kind of reputation you

Special People

There was a time not

long ago when being

Native wasn't so special.

◄ Danny Hewson visits the village graveyard, where many generations of Tsimshian ancestors are buried.

Traditions

A number of contemporary Tsimshian are working to restore their traditions, such as potlatching, dancing, language, and art.

▲ ARTIST WAYNE HEWSON PAINTS A STYLIZED DESIGN ON HIS YELLOW CEDAR CARVING OF A SALMON.

▶ SUNSET ON ANNETTE ISLAND.

get, deserved or not, is difficult to shake. I am gratified, though, that through perseverance, the journey these days is smoother and better understood by the people I love dearly, and I continue to strive to present Tsimshian and Native culture in the best way possible. How we live, whether it be as Native people looking to be good role models for the next generation, or just as good human beings expecting the same from others, will come back to us.

I am thrilled to see my masks and designs danced and drummed on, and used for what they were meant for. I am happy that I have been able to make a positive mark on my own people, my sons, and others who will take the art and the songs to the next generation. Yet I know we are hard on each other. Native people, I mean. We can be harder than any outsider could be. We need to praise and support each other. When one succeeds, all succeed.

There was a time not long ago when being Native wasn't so special. Outsiders judged and condemned us. Consequently, a lot of what made us unique almost went away—the language, the potlatch, the arts, the community. But now, no one is telling us "no." Only our own actions will determine the future.

What comes back to us.

David Boxley is a Tsimshian carver from Metlakatla, Alaska, who now lives in Kingston, Washington. In all of his works of art, from totem poles to box drums to prints, he emphasizes Tsimshian style. He has been deeply involved in the rebirth of Tsimshian culture through organizing and hosting potlatches in Alaska and Washington State. He has written more than twenty-five songs and carved more than thirty masks for Tsimshian Haayuuk, the dance group he leads in Seattle. He also started a dance group in Metlakatla.

SIBERIAN YUPIK

Savoonga is a Siberian Yupik Eskimo village of about six hundred fifty people located on St. Lawrence Island in the northern Bering Sea. The island is treeless and windswept, and yet what may seem harsh and uninviting to the stranger is beloved to the people who live there year-round. The sea provides sustenance; flights from Nome, one hundred thirty miles away on the mainland, bring supplemental groceries and other supplies.

St. Lawrence Island is ninety-five miles long and twenty-five miles wide. A second major community on the island is Gambell, with six hundred fifty people. Smaller camps dot the island, places where people travel seasonally for fishing and hunting marine mammals.

Siberian Yupik people are distinct from other Alaska Eskimos, with a language and traditions more similar to those of their ancestral kin: Eskimos who live on the Chukchi Peninsula in Siberia. Before the Cold War and the "Ice Curtain" that fell across the Pacific Ocean, people on both sides of the Bering Strait traveled across for visits in large skin boats. For forty years, friends and families were separated by international politics, but now visiting has resumed.

The Siberian Yupik Eskimos on St. Lawrence Island share language and customs with the Russian communities of Chaplino (New Chaplino) and Sighinek (Sireniki).

Take Care of Others—
You Cannot Live without Them

◆

GEORGE NOONGWOOK

◉

My given name is Mangtaquli, after one of my forefathers. I was born here in Savoonga in 1949 and have lived most of my life here except for the mid-1960s to the early 1970s, when I was away at boarding high school and in the military.

▲ IN SAVOONGA, THE ADAGE "IT TAKES A VILLAGE TO RAISE A CHILD" IS STILL AT WORK.

◄ THE OLD VILLAGE OF POOWOOILIAK OVERLOOKS THE BERING SEA.

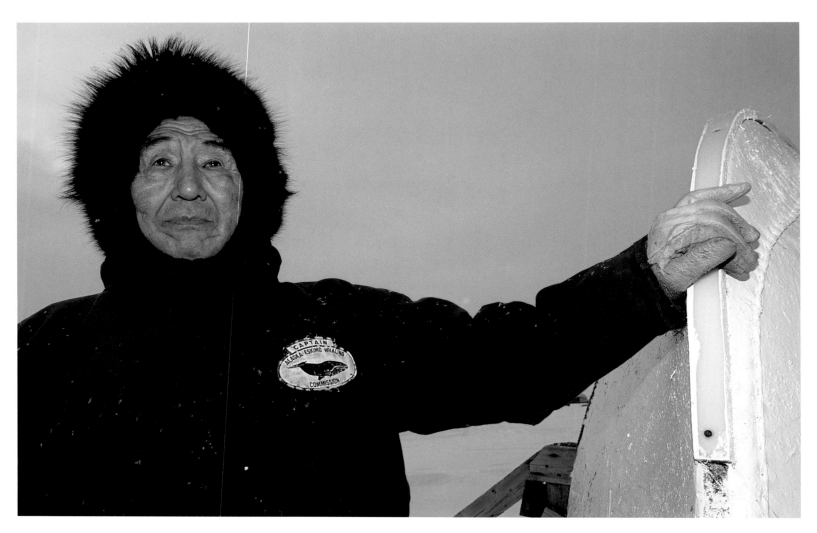

"Sivuqaq"

It literally means "to squeeze the water out of cloth or something." It is said that the land was picked up from beneath the sea and water squeezed out to form this island.

St. Lawrence Island is called Sivuqaq in our language. It literally means "to squeeze the water out of cloth or something." It is said that the land was picked up from beneath the sea and water squeezed out to form this island, and it is shaped to fit the palm of a hand.

From the time I became aware of my surroundings, there were people taking care of me, most notably my grandfather, Nunguk, who died when I was only seven years old. It seemed as though we were always doing things together such as gathering wood, fishing, making things out of ivory to trade for goods from the local store, playing, and visiting other people, especially my maternal grandparents, whose people were from across the Bering Strait. They and their children had nothing but love and goodies to shower me with, and I would often ask my grandfather when we were going to *pangeghta*, or visit our Chukotkan relatives across the water in Russia. Then one day, just like that, my grandfather was gone from my life.

◄▲ CHESTER NOONGWOOK, WHALING CAPTAIN.

◄ COLLIN NOONGWOOK PAUSES BY A SKIN BOAT, CALLED AN *UMIAK*, WHICH IS MADE FROM WALRUS HIDE STRETCHED OVER A WOODEN FRAME.

▲ A LACK OF PLUMBING NECESSITATES THE USE OF "HONEY BUCKETS"; VILLAGERS CARRY OUT THEIR WASTE WATER, EVEN IN BLIZZARD CONDITIONS.

▲ Parsons Noongwook smiles with satisfaction after a fifty-mile journey across St. Lawrence Island to finally reach whaling camp at Poowooiliak.

▶▲ Raymond Toolie, left, and Ron Toolie prepare to unhitch a skin boat from a sled, which was towed overland from Savoonga to whaling camp.

▶ Collin Noongwook, right, stops to rest with traveling companions.

The loss of my grandfather was difficult for me; but other people also spent time with me, and they must have loved me very much to spend so much time with me and take care of me. My uncle, my father's brother, Qagughmii, began to take me along with him on his excursions. We went by dogsled during July to our fish camp to set net and seine for arctic char and lake trout. He and one of his boys, usually Dwight, would come along on our outings. The trips were work, mostly. I remember walking along the dry tundra with a load of fish and getting very tired. I didn't mind because the fish provided much-needed protein to a lot of other people who spent time with me, and they let me know they appreciated the fish that we brought home.

As we continued these fishing trips, I soon realized that I was not getting tired as much, and the challenge became enjoyable. I loved the beauty of the country, the wildlife, the rivers and lakes full of fish, and the fact that all of it was there for me to enjoy with very few people around. I usually had such a good time that I didn't realize that I was very wet, cold, and tired.

Some of my favorite memories of spending time with family members are from spring. One time I went out with my Uncle Nathan, his boys, and others on a walrus hunt in "our" skin boat, built by my grandfather or one of my granduncles. I remember a Bering Sea as flat as glass and a full-blast spring sun on a herd of walrus resting on top of the ice. They stank to high heaven, they made horrible grunting sounds, and they were frightening when I first saw them. I would much rather have been elsewhere, but when I saw the excitement and happiness on the faces of my uncle and his boys, my fear ebbed a little. They shot a few animals, and as we began to clean and butcher the

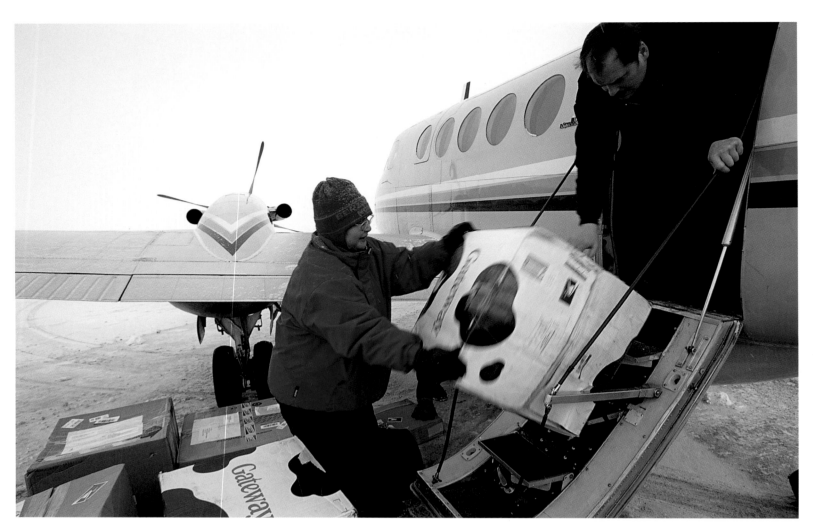

Caring

From the time I became aware, there were people taking care of me . . . my maternal grandparents had nothing but love and goodies to shower me with.

walruses, I felt the camaraderie and elation flowing from every one of my family members. We all knew that, through this hunt, we were taking care of our village, that our women, children, and other community members would partake of the fruits of our labor. Even our dogs, which were waiting on the shore-fast ice to take us and the walrus meat home to our families, would feast.

When the weather wasn't ideal for hunting, some of the men would get together to exchange ideas, stories, or to recap their hunting expeditions. Part of the conversation was about the hazards encountered during recent experiences, and in this way, others learned. Some lessons were learned in a humorous way. For instance, there might be a discussion about a specific individual who did something he shouldn't have and learned his lesson the hard way. Most of the down time was spent singing and dancing at

◄▲ BERING AIR AGENT, ROSEMARY AKEYA, UNLOADS BOXES OF COMPUTERS AND OTHER FREIGHT.

◄▼ A FAMILY HEADS HOME BY SNOWMACHINE AFTER SHOPPING AT THE STORE NEARLY DRIFTED OVER WITH SNOW.

▲ OUT ON A SLED RIDE, A BABY IN A WARM, FUR-RUFFED PARKA IS UNFAZED BY THE BLIZZARD BLOWING AT HER BACK.

Community

I was taught to practice care,

because you can't truly live

without people you care about.

◄ THE REMAINS OF A SLED AND
CASKET AT A GRAVESITE IN THE HILLS
ABOVE GAMBELL.

105

▲ SHIRLENE APASSINGOK PICKS ROSEROOT
GREENS ALONG A SUNNY HILLSIDE.

someone's home, and just by watching and listening, I picked up some of the songs that were being sung.

When I grew older and had a family of my own, I was invited one day to come and sing with our group of local singers. I recognized some but not all of the songs they were singing. They would sing a song and repeat it again and again until I was able to sing along, and then they would move on to the next song; but they would first explain to me who made the song, where it was made, and for what purpose. I later learned they thought that I had the natural ability to sing and to remember their songs, and they were enhancing my talents by teaching me songs. They spent a lot of time with me because after we finished one session, we would do it all over again at someone

▲ Anders Apassingok selects roseroot greens to be eaten later with whale or walrus meat.

◄ Parakeet auklets are prized and hunted along cliffsides.

▲ MERLE APASSINGOK, IVORY CARVER.

►FROM LEFT, LINONET AQELQAQ, CHESTER NOONGWOOK, AND NATASHA TATAPIA. WHILE CONVERSING IN SIBERIAN YUPIK DURING THIS SITTING, THE TRIO LEARNED THAT THEY ARE RELATED. AQELQAQ AND TATAPIA WERE VISITING FROM THE SIBERIAN TOWN OF PROVIDENYA.

else's home. To this day, I really do have a passion for St. Lawrence–style singing and dancing, which we do here almost every weekend. I know whose song I'm singing, where it came from, and for what reason. Watching other community members' faces light up when I begin to sing "their" songs is a real joy.

Because others took care of me and taught me in a caring way, I am able to pass on Yupik values to my children and to others in my community. I really enjoy spending a lot of time with my children and, now that I am a grandfather, my two grandchildren. I was taught to love and care about my children with all my heart, as if today were the last day I could be with them. I was taught to practice care, because you can't truly live without people you care about, and to grab the moment. When that moment has passed, you can say that you truly spent care and love, and you'll never feel sorry for having done so.

▲ DELMA APASSINGOK CUTS A SNACK OF WHALE MEAT FOR DAUGHTER, JANI, AS HUSBAND, EDMOND, TALKS ON THE PHONE.

▶ ▶ AN ORANGE SUN SETS THE SKY ABLAZE IN ITS RETREAT BEYOND THE SIBERIAN COAST.

George Noongwook, a Siberian Yupik Eskimo, is a lifelong resident of St. Lawrence Island and one of twenty-eight registered whaling captains in the village of Savoonga. He is president of the Savoonga Whaling Captains Association and a commissioner on the Alaska Eskimo Whaling Commission. His family comes from the Pugughileq (southwest cape of St. Lawrence Island) and his clan is Pugughileghmii. He and his wife, Jeanie, live with their three children and two grandchildren.

H A I D A

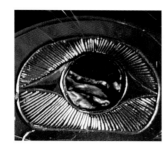

Home for Alaska's Haida people lies on the lower half of Prince of Wales Island at the southern tip of the Alaska Panhandle. This Native group crosses international boundaries, with traditional lands in Canada's Queen Charlotte Islands. Stories are told about lean times in the Queen Charlottes long ago and about how some Haida people gained permission from a Tlingit chief to settle on a portion of Prince of Wales, where fish and game were plentiful; other stories speak of war between the two peoples and that the Haida laid claim to this portion of the island.

About six hundred Haida live in Alaska today, and many still rely on fish and land animals as the mainstays of their diets. Commercial and subsistence fishing remains an important part of the Haida lifestyle.

Giant canoes carved from single, massive trees of the Queen Charlotte Islands were the traditional hallmark of these seafaring people. Totems, masks, and complex panels continue to display the talents of skilled carvers. Haida artisans are also known for their work with silver jewelry as well as argillite, a shiny, black stone.

Only a handful of people still speak the Haida language. As with the Tlingit and Tsimshian peoples, traditional society is organized into moieties, clans, and sub-clans. Potlatches are celebrated with singing and dancing, important ceremonies, feasting, gift giving, and remembering aloud the people of the past and their deeds.

Share What You Have—
Giving Makes You Richer

◆

JEANE BREINIG

◉

My mother, Julie Jones Coburn, turned eighty this summer. She is one of only about ten remaining speakers of the Alaskan Haida language. She was born and raised in Kasaan, one of two Haida villages left in Alaska out of four in the

▲ MICKEY CALHOUN JR. PREFERS A TRADITIONAL SPRUCE-BARK HAT FOR DAILY WEAR.

◄ HYDABURG'S TOTEM POLE PARK IS SITUATED NEXT DOOR TO THE VILLAGE SCHOOL.

Carving

Totems, masks, and complex panels continue to display the talents of skilled carvers.

▲ A ROW OF TOTEM POLES REPRESENTS
THE HAIDA CLANS.

► ▲ HAIDA JEWELRY AND A RATTLE BEAR
THE CLAN SYMBOLS.

► EARLY HAIDA SILVERSMITHS RECYCLED
U.S. QUARTERS INTO WORKS OF ART.
THESE CONTEMPORARY PIECES WERE
CREATED MORE CONVENTIONALLY.

world—the other three being Hydaburg in Alaska, and Masset and Skidegate in the Queen Charlotte Islands in Canada. Growing up just after the time of overt Haida language suppression, she says that she always understood Haida because it was the primary language spoken by her parents at home. But her mother and father, my grandmother and grandfather (*náan* and *chan*), wanted their children to speak to them in English because they realized their children would be living in a much-changed world, one in which English-language fluency had become an economic and practical necessity. My mother tells me that as a child she always understood Haida, but was not a fluent speaker.

When she was in her late thirties she made a concentrated effort to relearn our language. During the 1970s, concerned Southeast Alaskan Haida worked with linguists

▲ AT NINETY-FOUR, ESTHER NIX IS THE
OLDEST PERSON LIVING IN HYDABURG.

► LAVERNE EDENSHAW AND SON, MICHAEL, AT
THE ENTRANCE TO SUKKWAN STRAIT. CLAN
MEMBERSHIP IS PASSED FROM MOTHER TO
CHILD IN THIS MATRIARCHAL SOCIETY.

to create a writing system. Out of this came the first Alaska Haida books written in
both Haida and English. Then the language really re-bloomed for my mom, and she
made up her mind to speak Haida every day of her life and to pass on as much as she
could. I'm proud of her and grateful. Because of her foresight and generosity, I now
speak and understand a bit more Haida than if she hadn't done this.

Years later, my mother also began writing in English the things she said she wanted
her children and grandchildren to know about their history and genealogy, along with
memories of life in Kasaan as she knew it. She wrote more than sixty pages by hand,
and I helped her type them. Through this we laughed and grew closer, and I learned
more about her and how life used to be in our village. Recently, some of this writing
was published in *Alaska Native Writers, Storytellers and Orators: The Expanded Edition* (1999).
The gift she has given our family, and now to the world through publication, inspires
me and reminds me of one of our important Haida traditions based upon giving. It also
reminds me that although much has changed in our world, there are ways we can support and nurture our cultural traditions today; through this we will all be enriched.

We Haida are a small group among other Alaska Natives. There are perhaps six
hundred to seven hundred of us living in Alaska, with more scattered across the Lower
48 states. Many of us no longer live in our original villages. After contact with
European immigrants, our population was decimated by diseases such as smallpox,
tuberculosis, and influenza, to which we had little resistance. Some accounts place the
population loss at 90 percent of an estimated original Haida population (including

Enrichment

Although much has changed in our world, there are ways we can support and nurture our cultural traditions today; through this we will all be enriched.

Canadian Haida) of about ten thousand. Our survival depended upon adaptation to a changing world, and sharing is one important tradition we can still pass along.

Many people are familiar with the Northwest Coast "potlatch," a huge gift-exchange system between two opposite clans and an important part of Haida life much commented on by the people who first encountered us. This tradition demonstrates quite literally how "giving makes you richer." For example, first one clan would host an elaborate potlatch for the opposite clan, whose members were considered the guests. Food gathering, and making or bartering enough gifts to give way, could take a year or more as the whole clan worked to accumulate the necessary goods. The result of this would be a huge ceremonial event during which stories would be told, dances performed, names bestowed, honors given, and, of course, the fruits of all the hard work would be distributed to the opposite clan. The next time, it would be the opposite

◄▲ SILVER BRACELETS AND RING BEARING HAIDA CLAN SYMBOLS ADORN A GIRL'S HAND.

◄ SILVERSMITH WARREN PEALE AT WORK ON A BRACELET IN HIS STUDIO.

▲ BECKY FRANK WEAVES CEDAR BARK BASKETS AND HATS AT HER DINING ROOM TABLE.

Harvest of the Sea

Traditional foods connect us to our past, to our cultural identity, and to each other.

clan's responsibility to host the event, with an obligation to give even more, and so on, in a never-ending cycle.

While Haida potlatches of this magnitude are not common in Alaska today, exchange and sharing still are. You can see this most clearly as it applies to our traditional foods, which connect us to our past, to our cultural identity, and to each other. Food gathering on the lands and waterways of Southeast Alaska has always been an important part of life for the Haida, Tlingit, and Tsimshian peoples who live here. Seaweed and herring-egg gathering, salmon and halibut fishing, clam digging, berry picking, deer hunting, and smoking and preserving our foods highlight an important aspect of life we still enjoy and one that connects us to our past in tangible ways. Food gathering also gives us a chance to share what we get with family members who may now live far away and are unable to gather the food themselves. This brings us closer together.

In Alaska, "food gathering" has become commonly known as "subsistence," an unfortunate term that doesn't really get at the heart of what traditional foods mean to Native peoples. "Subsistence" suggests living hand to mouth, perhaps barely even clinging to physical survival. While many "bush" Alaskans (Native and non-Native

◄▲ CLIFTON CARLE PREPARES TO HEAD FOR THE SHRIMP GROUNDS.

◄ GERARD HELGESEN JR. EN ROUTE TO CRABBING WATERS IN SUKKWAN STRAIT.

▲ GERARD HELGESEN HAULS A DAY'S CATCH OF SHRIMP FROM SOUTH PASS.

Potlatch

Giving makes us richer because through it we come to understand how our lives have been built on the generosity of our relations and ancestors.

◄ A MASSIVE TOTEM POLE STANDS IN FRONT OF A RESTORED LONGHOUSE IN THE OLD VILLAGE OF KASAAN.

alike) living in remote villages with few economic opportunities depend on the land's natural resources for a crucial part of their physical sustenance, food gathering provides more than nutrition for Native peoples. Food gathering gives us a concrete way to keep us connected to our traditions. For example, learning how to gather and prepare the foods means working closely with our families, who have knowledge to share. Through this we learn more about who we are and how we are connected to our traditional homelands. In truth, gathering, preparing, and eating our traditional foods connect us to our ancestors in emotional and spiritual ways and remind us of life's abundance and the blessings it bestows on us.

Because we are blessed, we also have a responsibility to give where we can, to pass on what we know, and to adapt when necessary while remaining true to our cultural values. My mother's work with Haida-language and English-language writing is a good example and an inspiration.

I also like to remember my *chan*, Louis Lear Jones, a remarkable man who was raised for part of his life in a traditional Haida longhouse. He married my grandmother in one of the last arranged Haida marriages, yet lived to hear the radio broadcast of the first man walking on the moon. He witnessed an astonishing number of changes during his life and through it all kept a strong spirit. His experience as a boat builder provides

► AFTER SELECTING A SUITABLE TREE, POWELL CHARLES CUTS FIREWOOD.

a good example. Haida people have earned a reputation as some of the world's finest wood-carvers, and this skill is still being taught in its traditional form, with new Haida artisans emerging with regularity. Among some of their more famous works are spectacular seagoing, dugout canoes carved from cedar logs. My grandfather carried on and adapted this tradition to meet his family's needs, and to adapt to a rapidly changing world. After the influx of non-Natives into Southeast Alaska, the traditional fishing, hunting, and gathering activities of Natives began to be supplemented by a cash economy. My *chan* raised his family in Kasaan about the time commercial fishing had developed as an industry here. Realizing the value of his sons having their own fishing boats, he ordered blueprints from the back of a magazine and became a self-taught boat builder. With this knowledge, he built forty-foot-plus seine vessels that he eventually gave to his sons.

In truth, giving makes us richer because through it we come to understand how our lives have been built on the generosity of our relations and ancestors.

▲ A SUNNY DAY FINDS MICKEY CALHOUN JR. WALKING HIS DOG IN HYDABURG.

Jeane Breinig is Haida (Raven, Brown Bear, Taaslaanas Clan) and originally from Kasaan village in Southeast Alaska. She holds a doctorate in English (American and Native American Literary Studies) from the University of Washington. Breinig coedited Alaska Native Writers, Storytellers and Orators: The Expanded Edition *(1999) and is currently working on a Kasaan Haida Elders' interview project. She is an associate professor of English at the University of Alaska Anchorage.*

E Y A K

The Eyak people of Southcentral Alaska are the fewest in number of any Native group within Alaska. Traditionally, they fished and hunted in the great Copper River Delta, in the vast forests and along the coast of Prince William Sound. The people lived between two great powers, the Athabascan Indians to the north and west, and the Tlingit to the east and southeast. Aleut and Chugach (Alutiiq) people also dwelt along the western shores of Prince William Sound. While retaining their own unique identity, the Eyaks, like other border people, traded and adapted certain customs and tools from their neighbors. Linguistically, they are linked to both the Athabascans and the Tlingit, but culturally, they are more like the Southeast Native people groups. The Eyaks are divided into moieties and clans with bird or animal figures as their totems. They were the northernmost Native group to carve totem poles. Although totem carving is no longer practiced, a couple of historical images of Eyak poles remain.

Many contemporary Eyaks live in or near Cordova, on the Copper River Delta. Commercial and subsistence fishing remains important, not only to physical survival but as a cultural expression and a tangible link to their past. Of the one hundred forty remaining Eyak people, only one speaks the traditional language.

Know Who You Are—You Are a Reflection on Your Family

◆

DUNE LANKARD

◉

As a young boy in the late 1960s, I realized I was entering a time of great change for the land and for our Eyak people. Through the eyes of my grandmother, Lena Ahtahkee Saska, and my mother, Rosie Lankard, I was witnessing the beginnings

▲ HONORARY CHIEF MARIE SMITH-JONES IS THE LAST SPEAKER OF THE EYAK LANGUAGE.

◀ MOST OF THE VESSELS IN THE CORDOVA HARBOR ARE WORKING BOATS THAT SUPPORT COMMERCIAL FISHING IN PRINCE WILLIAM SOUND.

◄ JOE COOK HEADS OUT TO THE COPPER RIVER DELTA ON OPENING DAY OF THE RED SALMON SEASON. "I'LL TELL YOU ONE THING," HE SAYS. "I'M COMMERCIAL FISHING ON MY ANCESTRAL HOMELAND."

▲ IN KEEPING WITH TRADITION, COOK GIVES AWAY A SHARE OF HIS SALMON FROM HIS BOAT, THE F/V *BELEN-C*.

of the Alaska Native Claims Settlement Act (ANCSA, 1971). Ever since the time we were young pups, we seven siblings heard from Mom and Grandma that Eyaks were special and different from all the other Native people in Cordova. We didn't know exactly what all that meant, but we were soon to find out.

As children, we took turns accompanying Ahtahkee to visit her Native elder women friends who lived in what was once our last village site in "old town" Cordova. Ahtahkee spoke in three different languages (Eyak, Aleut, and English) with her friends. Often their topics of conversation ranged from federal land claims in Alaska to subsistence, sovereignty, and spirituality. The elder women shared their knowledge of the seasons of animals that migrated each year through Prince William Sound and the Copper River Delta. They told us where and when to go get the animals, hooligan, salmon, berries, and other staples of our subsistence diet. Ahtahkee and Mom would share legends and tell us how our proud, yet tiny, Eyak Nation survived between the powerful seafaring tribes of Tlingit, Chugach, and Aleut Nations. And, they would tell me that one day I would have to defend and protect our people and way of life.

The Eyaks appear to have migrated from Interior Alaska to the coast perhaps three thousand years ago. The Russian invasion into Alaska a couple of centuries ago probably did the Eyaks little or no harm. The Russians did, however, recognize the Eyaks and our unique language on their fur-trading maps. When the Americans intruded into local history, that is ironically what probably saved the Eyaks from final assimilation by the Tlingit. We were between a rock and a hard place.

For many, many generations the Tlingit and the minority Eyaks more or less accepted each other because we had some of the same cultural traditions. But the Eyaks lived precariously between the Tlingit to the south and the Chugach Eskimo Natives

Moieties and clans

The Eyaks are divided into moieties and clans with bird or animal figures as their totems.

to the west. Eyaks were outnumbered, and had we not gone along with our Tlingit allies, we might have been erased from living memory. Our Eyak language and culture were in danger of complete Tlingit assimilation when, in 1889, the first American canneries were established in our Eyak territory. The canneries hired Chinese and American male laborers who brought alcohol, opium, disease, and violence to our people. Out of the a population of three hundred Eyaks at the time, more than two-thirds perished in just a matter of twenty or so years. The new residents also depleted resources. They fished greedily with traps and dynamite, destroying our salmon subsistence lifestyle and uprooting us from our traditional homelands.

The City of Cordova was incorporated in 1906 to create the ocean terminus for the Copper River & Northwestern Railway, which was completed in 1911. It ran up the Copper River to Kennecott, site of what was the richest copper mine in the world.

▲ THE KING SALMON OF THE COPPER RIVER ARE SOUGHT-AFTER BY RESTAURATEURS ACROSS THE COUNTRY; FEW DINERS ARE AWARE OF ITS ENORMOUS PROPORTIONS.

▲ IRENE WOODS PRESERVES
FIREWEED HONEY.

▶ JENNA MAY IS AN IMPRESSIONIST
WHO GAINS INSPIRATION FROM THE
SURROUNDING LANDSCAPE.

The land claims rush was on. While the Alaganik Eyaks were being nearly wiped out by epidemics, the remaining Eyak survivors fled from Eyak River to the western end of Eyak Lake in old town Cordova. By 1933, there were only perhaps thirty-something Eyaks alive. At that time, anthropologist Frederica deLaguna realized our language was unique, and so we Eyaks became the last Indian Nation in North America to be "recognized" by the American government. DeLaguna wrote a book about the Eyak situation titled *The Eyak Indians of the Copper River Delta*. She wrote that she feared the Eyaks were about to go extinct.

By the late 1960s, Native and non-Native people with briefcases came often to our house to talk with Ahtahkee and Mom about how the Eyaks needed to participate and help organize the Native land settlement for our region. Ahtahkee would always get angry and say, "They're here to take our land, not give it back to us!" We would say, "Grandma, they are here to help us get our land claims." She would growl, because she knew better. The bureaucrats would stay and talk for hours about how we would finally receive land and money. They would tell us how our lives would be better because we would finally be in control of our land and our own destiny. We would listen and watch and look for signs of truth in their eyes, gestures, and words. I would try to listen with my heart and not my mind so much, because I wanted to believe that it was all true and that we would have our Eyak village again, someday soon.

The settlement act of 1971 defined new land boundaries and determined who would receive shares in these new "Native corporations." Unlike indigenous people in the Lower 48 who were placed on reservations, Alaska Natives were forced to create American for-profit corporations in order to receive land claims from the federal government.

▲ Faye Pahl's Eyak name is "Tanakamaa," which means "eggs from the fish." She was born after her mother ate a meal of herring eggs.

▶▲ The Copper River Delta is a major rest stop for migrating shorebirds; each spring Cordova hosts a festival to celebrate their return. Shown here are western sandpipers and dunlins.

▶ A trumpeter swan.

Alaska Natives who proved they possessed at least one-quarter Native blood, regardless of ancestral region or tribal status, would receive one hundred shares of common stock from one of the twelve "regional corporations" throughout the state. (One other, called The Thirteenth Corporation, was based in the Pacific Northwest for Alaska Natives living in the Lower 48 states.) And if you could meet the requirements for membership in one of the two hundred twenty "village corporations," you were to receive one hundred shares in that, plus land and potential money settlements.

In much conflict, Ahtahkee, my mother, and other living Eyak legends testified in court, expressing the history of the minority Eyak people and identifying place names of ancestry and subsistence territories from Yakutat to Cordova, a three-hundred-mile stretch of coastal habitat. Ahtahkee knew that without her testimony and that of others proving traditional Native inhabitation of the region, it was possible that the Bureau of Indian Affairs (BIA) could approve a determination of Eyak extinction. Then all the Natives at that time in the traditional Eyak region of Cordova—Aleut, Tlingit, Chugach Eskimo, and Eyaks—might have been designated "at-large shareholders." They would not be eligible for village corporation membership and thus would remain landless.

Ahtahkee passed away before ANCSA swept up her land and before some of her fears came true. In 1974, three years after ANCSA's passage, the Eyaks were to be the final recognized, independent, and separate tribal nation in Alaska entitled to land claims. From the very first day, however, the Eyaks became a "super-minority" tribal shareholder of their own land-claims village corporation. Only 25 of the 326 Eyak Corporation shareholders are of true Eyak descent. Most are Aleut. These others have often made decisions to log, mine, drill, and sell our ancestral land.

Preservation

We hope that now is the time when we can heal the past and find ways to encourage all families and all peoples to live harmoniously together with our sacred land and water.

► EYAK ACTIVIST DUNE LANKARD POSES WITH A FALLEN OLD-GROWTH TREE IN PRINCE WILLIAM SOUND. HE WAS ONCE NAMED *TIME* MAGAZINE'S "HERO OF THE PLANET" FOR SINGLE-HANDEDLY STOPPING LOGGING IN PRINCE WILLIAM SOUND.

▲ SIXTEEN-YEAR-OLD DIANA REIDEL WORKS WITH SEA OTTER PELTS TO MAKE HATS, PARKAS, AND MITTENS.

▶ SKIN-SEWERS MONICA REIDEL, LEFT, AND HER DAUGHTER, DIANA, MODEL THE PARKAS AND HAT THAT THEY FASHIONED FROM SEAL, OTTER, AND WOLF FURS.

When the nation's worst oil spill happened in our backyard in 1989, we Eyaks were able to preserve our ancestral lands around Cordova and the Sound from being clear-cut by using the Exxon Valdez Oil Spill Restoration Fund—though, considering the oil's damage, the settlement was bittersweet. We hope that now is the time when we can heal the past and find ways to encourage all families and all peoples in the Prince William Sound and Copper River Delta region to live harmoniously together with our sacred land and water.

Today, only one living speaker of our Eyak language remains. Her name is Marie Smith-Jones. She is eighty-three years old and our honorary Chief. Her family is from the Raven moiety along the Eyak River. Scatterings of Eyaks remain alive—approximately one hundred forty Eyaks exist around Alaska and the United States. Some of us, like my sister Pamela Smith, continue the wonderful old ways of a subsistence lifestyle, harvesting the wild salmon and berries, the good food that keeps us alive and restores our Eyak spirit. May the wild places—living monuments—remain wild and free, and may the spirit of the Eyaks live on forever.

There are not many of us, but we know who we are.

Glen Dune Lankard is an Eyak Athabascan Native from the Eagle moiety at Alaganik. Dune's Eyak name is Jamachakih, which means "little bird that screams really loud and won't shut up." He continues in his efforts to preserve and restore his Eyak culture and ancestral lands in the Copper River Delta region and to bring attention to environmental issues through his non-profit organization called Red Zone.

Recommended Reading

Andrews, Susan B., and John Creed, eds. *Authentic Alaska: Voices of Its Native Writers*. Lincoln, Nebr.: University of Nebraska Press, 1998.

Apassingok, Anders, Willis Walunga, Raymond Oozevaseuk, and Edward Tennant, eds. *Sivuqam Nangaghnegha Siivanllemta: Lore of St. Lawrence Island, Echoes of our Eskimo Elders*. Vol. 2. Unalakleet, Alaska: Bering Strait School District, 1987.

Barker, James. *Always Getting Ready, Upterrlainarluta: Yup'ik Eskimo Subsistence in Southwest Alaska*. Seattle: University of Washington Press, 1993.

Beck, Mary Giraudo. *Potlatch: Native Ceremony and Myth on the Northwest Coast*. Seattle: Alaska Northwest Books, 1993.

Brown, Emily Ivanoff. *Tales of Ticasuk*. Fairbanks: University of Alaska Press, 1987.

Brown, Tricia. Photography by Roy Corral. *Children of the Midnight Sun: Young Native Voices of Alaska*. Seattle: Alaska Northwest Books, 1998.

Bruchac, Joseph, ed. *Raven Tells Stories: An Anthology of Alaska Native Writing*. Greenfield, N.Y.: The Greenfield Review Press, 1991.

Burch, Ernest S., Jr. *The Iñupiaq Eskimo Nations of Northwest Alaska*. Fairbanks: University of Alaska Press, 1998.

Chisholm, Colin. *Through Yup'ik Eyes*. Portland, Oregon: Alaska Northwest Books, 2000.

Dauenhauer, Nora Marks, and Richard Dauenhauer, eds. *Haa Shuká, Our Ancestors: Tlingit Oral Narratives*. Seattle: University of Washington Press, 1987.

___. *Haa Kusteeyí, Our Culture: Tlingit Life Stories*. Seattle: University of Washington Press, 1994.

Dmytryshyn, Basil, E. A. P. Crownhart-Vaughan, and Thomas Vaughan. *The Russian American Colonies: A Documentary Record, 1798-1867*. Portland, Oregon: Oregon Historical Society, 1989.

Eastman, Carol M., and Elizabeth A. Edwards. *Gyaehlingaay: Traditions, Tales and Images of the Kaigani Haida*. Seattle: University of Washington Press, 1991.

Fienup-Riordan, Ann. *Boundaries and Passages, Rule and Ritual in Yup'ik Eskimo Oral Tradition*. Norman, Okla.: University of Oklahoma Press, 1994.

Fienup-Riordan, Ann, William Tyson, Paul John, and Marie Meade. *Hunting Tradition in a Changing World: Yup'ik Lives in Alaska Today*. Piscataway, N.J.: Rutgers University Press, 2000.

Fredson, John. *Hàa Googwandak: Stories Told by John Fredson to Edward Sapir*. Fairbanks: Alaska Native Language Center, 1982.

Freedman, Lew. *Spirit of the Wind: The Story of George Attla, Alaska's Legendary Sled Dog Sprint Champ*. Seattle: Epicenter Press, 2001.

Haines, Jan Harper. *Cold River Spirits: A Story of an Athabascan-Irish Family from Alaska's Yukon River*. Seattle: Epicenter Press, 2000.

Haycox, Stephen W., and Mary Childers Mangusso, eds. *An Alaska Anthology: Interpreting the Past*. Seattle: University of Washington Press, 1996.

Hudson, Ray. *Moments Rightly Placed: An Aleutian Memoir*. Seattle: Epicenter Press, 1999.

Huhndorf, Roy M. *Reflections on the Alaska Native Experience*. Anchorage: The CIRI Foundation, 2001.

Huntington, Sidney, as told to Jim Rearden. *Shadows on the Koyukuk: An Alaskan Native's Life Along the River*. Seattle: Alaska

Northwest Books, 1993.

Jans, Nick. *The Last Light Breaking: Living Among Alaska's Inupiat Eskimos*. Seattle: Alaska Northwest Books, 1994.

Jonaitis, Aldona, Susan McInnis, and Alvin Amason. *Looking North: Art from the University of Alaska Museum*. Seattle: University of Washington Press, 1998.

Jones, Dorothy Knee. *A Century of Servitude: Pribilof Aleuts Under U.S. Rule*. Lanham, Md.: University Press of America, 1980.

Kari, James, and Alan Boraas, eds. *A Dena'ina Legacy K'tl'egh'I Sukdu: The Collected Writings of Peter Kalifornisky*. Fairbanks: Alaska Native Language Center, 1991.

Kittredge, Frances. Illustrated by Howard Rock. *Neeluk: An Eskimo Boy in the Days of the Whaling Ships*. Portland, Oregon: Alaska Northwest Books, 2001.

Kohlhoff, Dean. *When the Wind Was a River: Aleut Evacuation in World War II*. Seattle: University of Washington Press, 1995.

Krauss, Michael E. *Alaska Native Languages: Past, Present, and Future*. Fairbanks: Alaska Native Language Center, 1980.

____. *In Honor of Eyak: The Art of Anna Nelson Harry*. Fairbanks: Alaska Native Language Center, 1982.

Langdon, Steve. *The Native People of Alaska*. 3rd ed. Anchorage: Greatland Graphics, 1993.

Luke, Howard. *My Own Trail*. Edited by Jan Steinbright Jackson. Fairbanks: Alaska Native Knowledge Network, 1998.

McClanahan, A. J. *Growing Up Native in Alaska*. Anchorage: The CIRI Foundation, 2001.

McClanahan, Alexandra J. *Our Stories, Our Lives*. Anchorage: The CIRI Foundation, 1986.

____, ed. *A Reference in Time: Alaska Native History Day by Day*. Anchorage: The CIRI Foundation, 2001.

Meade, Marie, trans., and Ann Fienup-Riordan, ed. *Agayuliyararput Kegginaqut, Kangiit-llu, Our Way of Making Prayer: Yup'ik Masks and the Stories They Tell*.

Seattle: University of Washington Press, 1996.

Mendenhall, Hannah, Ruth Sampson, and Edward Tennant. *Uqaaqtuangich Inupiat: Lore of the Inupiat, the Elders Speak*. Vol. 1. Kotzebue, Alaska: Northwest Arctic Borough School District, 1989.

Mulcahy, Joanne B. and Gordon L. Pullar. *Birth and Rebirth on an Alaskan Island: The Life of an Alutiiq Healer*. Athens, Ga.: University of Georgia Press, 2001.

Nelson, Richard K. *Make Prayers to the Raven: A Koyukon View of the Northern Forest*. Chicago: University of Chicago Press, 1983.

Oman, Lela Kiana. *The Epic of Qayaq: The Longest Story Ever Told by My People*. Seattle: University of Washington Press, 1995.

Pete, Shem. *Shem Pete's Alaska: The Territory of the Upper Cook Inlet Dena'ina*. Compiled and edited by James Kari. Fairbanks: Alaska Native Language Center, 1987.

Spatz, Ronald, ed. *Alaska Quarterly Review*. Vol. 10, *Alaska Native Writers, Storytellers and Orators: The Expanded Edition*. Anchorage: University of Alaska Anchorage, 1999.

Steinbright, Jan. Photography by Clark James Mishler. *Qayaqs and Canoes: Native Ways of Knowing*. Anchorage: Alaska Native Heritage Center, 2001.

Tiulana, Paul, as told to Vivian Senungetuk. *A Place for Winter: Paul Tiulana's Story*. Anchorage: The CIRI Foundation, 2000.

Wallis, Velma. *Bird Girl and the Man who Followed the Sun: An Athabaskan Indian Legend from Alaska*. Seattle: Epicenter Press, 1996.

____. *Two Old Women: An Alaska Legend of Betrayal, Courage and Survival*. Seattle: Epicenter Press, 1993.

Wilder, Edna. *Once Upon an Eskimo Time: A year of Eskimo life before the white man came as told to me by my wonderful mother whose name was Nedercook*. Seattle: Alaska Northwest Books, 1988.

Index